About the Author

Phillip E. Carroll lives in Victoria, Australia, where he works as an IT and Systems Manager. He writes from lived experience, close observation, and careful research – the kind that involves knowing what a Pink Lady apple tastes like in February and how the law feels behind closed doors. *Her Honour's Path* is his debut novel: a story of quiet ambition, emotional discipline, and the subtle forces that shape how we live and lead. When he's not writing or working, Phillip enjoys good coffee, quiet mornings, and the overlooked details that often hold the most meaning.

Her Honour's Path

Phillip E Carroll

Her Honour's Path

Olympia Publishers
London

www.olympiapublishers.com
OLYMPIA PAPERBACK EDITION

A CIP catalogue record for this title is available from the British Library.

ISBN: 978-1-80603-190-0

This is a work of fiction.
Names, characters, places and incidents originate from the writer's imagination. Any resemblance to actual persons, living or dead, is purely coincidental.

First Published in 2026

Olympia Publishers
Tallis House
2 Tallis Street
London
EC4Y 0AB

Printed in Great Britain

Acknowledgements

To the people in my life who inspired the characters in this book – thank you. Your courage, flaws, humour, and heart gave shape to these pages. Some of you may recognise yourselves; others may never know the role you played. But each of you left a mark, and for that, I am deeply grateful.

To my friend Violetta – thank you for reading the early drafts and for your kind encouragement. I truly appreciated our conversations throughout the writing process.

Part I – Market Beginnings
The Law of Fruit

The concrete of the wholesale market was still wet from the early morning hose-down. Forklifts beeped in the distance, and seagulls circled above the tin-roofed stalls. Kimberly Doors, clipboard in hand and a canvas bag slung across her shoulder, stood beside her father as he bartered over a stack of banana trays.

Too much," she said plainly. "Navels are moving at two-fifty a kilo – that's fifteen a tray retail. We'll pay eleven, or we move on."

Inside the bag, secured discreetly to a loop on her belt, was fifteen hundred dollars in fifty-dollar notes – not for everything, but for when cash made the difference. Bundled tight with a rubber band, it rested against her hip like a quiet emblem of trust, flexibility, and readiness. Most orders went on account, but not all deals waited for paperwork. Sometimes it sealed a price before someone else stepped in. Sometimes it turned a vendor's maybe into a yes. She used it when it counted – and she knew when it counted.

She was fifteen and precise, writing out the orders in tidy rows as if they were court transcripts. The night before, she had sat at the kitchen bench, carefully drafting the list: eight sacks of potatoes, ten trays of apples, four boxes of tomatoes – noting the current market prices beside each. Her father stood nearby, slicing beans with quiet purpose.

"You're doing the lot now," he said without looking up. "Next year I'll be out there sipping tea while you run the show."

Kimberly smirked. "As long as you still carry the boxes."

He gave a small grunt, but there was pride behind it. "Just don't buy anything we can't sell."

"Wouldn't dream of it," she said.

She went line by line, double-checking quantities against the stock left in their cool room. A mistake meant overbuying – or worse, waste. Her father leaned on her judgment more each week, and she wanted to get it right. They were a team, like co-counsel at the bartering bench – he led the negotiations, spoke with vendors, and handled the rhythm of the deals. But Kimberly ran the numbers, spotted the margins and flagged the risks. He was the voice; she was the brief.

The goal was simple: get what they needed, get it fresh, and not spend a cent more than they had to. She wasn't just helping – she was advising.

Alongside the main list, she'd left a margin column titled *What If* – contingencies and fallback options in case a good buy came up. If a vendor offered an unexpected deal, she could calculate on the spot how much cash they had left to play with. Some weeks, if prices fell just right, they'd buy a few extra punnets of strawberries or a spare bucket of late basil. It made the place look fresh and gave them a quiet little win with the morning walkers. It was part accounting, part instinct – and her father trusted it completely.

"How much for those bananas?" he'd ask, and she'd glance down, do the maths in seconds, and give him a number.

Not just a daughter – an operator in the making.

Across the lane, a boy about her age jumped down from the back of a truck. He had the sturdy shoulders of someone who'd been lifting crates since primary school. Dust on his sleeves, a split apple in his hand, and a paperback novel – something legal, something Grisham – half-tucked into his back pocket.

He glanced her way, just once. Kimberly raised her chin slightly. Not a smile – not yet – but a spark of curiosity passed between them. She noticed his eyes, the calm in the way he moved, the quiet confidence of someone used to carrying weight.

Then he turned, boots scuffing the concrete, and joined the others by the loading bay.

Kimberly looked away – but not for long.

Later, as her father chatted with another grocer, Kimberly joined the short line at the café stall, getting tea for herself and coffee for Dad.

From the corner of her eye, she saw him again – the boy from the truck. Now closer. Dusty sleeves, takeaway coffee in one hand, and that same paperback novel – *Grisham* – tucked into his back pocket.

As he shifted his grip on the coffee, a split apple slipped from under his arm and hit the ground with a soft *thud*.

Kimberly stepped forward, scooped it up before it rolled away, and handed it back, saying, "You dropped your apple."

He blinked, surprised.

"You've got good reflexes," he said.

"You've got butterfingers," she replied, then smiled.

A beat. Then, "I've seen you here before. But not with that orchard logo."

Paul followed her gaze to the folded delivery docket in his hand, the orchard stamp barely visible.

"First time doing the run," he said. "Usually, it's my dad and older brother. He's been unwell, so… here I am."

Kimberly gave a small nod. "Well, your apples sell really well at our shop. Customers always ask when they're coming in."

That earned a faint smile. "Good to know."

She gestured toward his back pocket. "*The Pelican Brief?*"

"Guilty."

"Grisham's a good start," she said, sipping her tea. "But if you ever plan on practising law, you'll have to read the actual legislation first."

He looked at her, then chuckled. "Noted."

She offered her hand. "Kimberly. Brandon Park."

"Paul."

He raised his coffee in a mock toast. "Maybe one day we'll meet again – opposite sides of a courtroom."

"So long as it's not over apples."

They both laughed – not too much, just enough.

From the open window of the farm truck, a voice called out, "Let's go, mate! Need to be back on the farm by ten!"

He glanced toward the truck, then back at her with a reluctant smile. "Duty calls."

There was a pause – not awkward, not rushed – just full of something unspoken.

She lifted her hand in a wave. A soft, steady gesture. Not flirty. Not shy. Just warm.

He gave a nod – almost a bow – and jogged off toward the waiting truck, boots crunching over gravel. She stood there a moment longer, watching the truck pull away, dust trailing behind it.

She handed her father his coffee, now only just warm, and pulled the clipboard from under her arm. "Potatoes, apples, two trays of bananas," she murmured. "And fifty left over for eggs if Mr Kartzis still has any."

She moved toward the back wall of the market, where the vendor booths sat behind scratched perspex and rows of docket books. Her father joined her, a pen clipped to his collar. One by one, they reviewed the paperwork – each stallholder had issued a delivery docket, and Kimberly checked the quantities against her list. Eight sacks of potatoes? Tick. Four trays of bananas? Tick. She marked substitutions, noted overages, and initialled each sheet before handing it back.

Most vendors ran their accounts – the shop would settle up on Mondays – but Kimberly still carried that thick stack of fifties at her hip. Because sometimes, cash was currency in more ways than one. A bit extra could secure a crate of figs just ripening, or close a deal before another buyer walked over. She didn't flash it – just used it when the moment was right, like a barrister reaching for precedent.

They left the market at seven thirty. Back at Brandon Park, the shop was already open. Her mum was arranging bananas in the front crates, waving at familiar customers.

The cool room hummed softly around her, its air crisp with the scent of citrus and damp cardboard. Kimberly crouched at the back, in front of the old safe tucked beneath a shelf of celery and parsnips. She turned the dial with steady fingers and opened it to reveal the float tray – notes stacked in neat, descending order. From the money clip hooked to her belt, she retrieved the leftover cash from that morning's market run. She laid out the seven hundred dollars carefully, flattening each note before sliding it beneath the tray. The math balanced. She'd taken fifteen hundred dollars, spent eight hundred and brought back the rest.

Pulling the ledger into her lap, she updated the entries with clean strokes, then checked the lower compartment of the safe. Yesterday's takings were still sealed in their pouch, clearly labelled, untouched. No confusion. No mixing. Her father's rule was still gospel: *cash in, cash out*.

She paused, considering the week ahead. The stallholders had been restless – too much stone fruit ripening at once, a glut of late citrus, and whispers of unsold berries coming in from the peninsula. It had the feel of a Clearline Tuesday, the kind of morning where growers were desperate to move stock before it turned soft or unsellable. That's when the real bargains appeared – but only for those who were ready.

Cash buyers got the nod. No one wanted to fuss with accounts, invoices, or follow-ups. The stallholders wanted clean sales – money in hand, no names, no debt. If you hesitated, they moved to the next buyer. Kimberly knew better than to show up light. She flipped to the back of the ledger and wrote:

Need three thousand dollars for Clearline Tuesday – heavy stock, no accounts.

She underlined it once. No circle. No drama. Just a line.

The cool room was quiet again. She returned the ledger to its place, closed the safe, and rose to her feet. The staff were just beginning to open the shutters out front. The shop would run smoothly today. But Kimberly's work – real work – was already done, locked away and labelled.

Kimberly worked on uploading the truck with Brad and Angelo. There were no forklifts now – just crates, quick hands and the hard-backed strength of youth. Angelo didn't have the years, but he still had the muscle.

She didn't know what next Tuesday would bring exactly. But she'd be ready. The line was clear.

She worked until midday. Her chicken salad waited on the back bench. She ate with a soft smile, watching as a teenager bought a new CD across the walkway – something American, flashy, loud. For Kimberly, it was another kind of dreaming.

At one thirty, she was home. Nana was there, in her armchair, wrapped in a knitted shawl. Kimberly changed out of her dusty clothes, made tea and curled beside her grandmother. They laughed at old stories. Kimberly read a few chapters of a Grisham novel out loud. It wasn't school reading, but it fed something deeper – the shape of justice, the pull of right and wrong.

Dinner was simple, prepared by Kimberly. She plated a tray for Nana – meat, three veg, peeled fruit and tea. Set it just right. By seven, the house was quiet. Her parents were still at the shop. She washed up, checked the receipts, then went to her room. She switched on the radio, lay on her bed with a book open across her chest, and stared at the ceiling.

Orchard Roots

Kimberly didn't come from a family of lawyers. She came from early mornings, from produce crates and vinegar-wiped floors. Her father believed in honest weights and fair prices. Her mother believed in neat uniforms and strong tea. And Nana? Nana believed in Kimberly.

The decision to study law wasn't made in a single moment. It lived quietly in her – somewhere between the 'What If' margins on the clipboard and the way she watched people when they didn't know they were being watched.

She had the grades for Melbourne. But she chose Monash. It was closer to home, and she couldn't imagine leaving Nana, not after everything. Thursday nights, Saturday mornings – she still worked at the shop. Her mother would press a sandwich into her hand as she raced for the bus, legal texts in one arm, a paper bag of mandarins in the other.

At Monash, she kept to herself mostly. Sat near the front. Took notes like she was being paid.

That's where she first noticed James Brady. He arrived late to almost every lecture, parking his VR Commodore too close to the kerb and walking in like he belonged everywhere. Still Xavier at heart, collar loose, hair slightly too long, preaching causes he only half-read. There was something reckless about him – all charm and contradiction. He called himself a rebel, but everyone knew his father was a senior partner at Brady, Sanderson and Associates.

Kimberly shouldn't have liked him. But something about the way he challenged every lecturer, the way he turned every tutorial into a stage – it got her attention.

One Thursday afternoon, she saw him standing on a planter box outside the library, speaking to a loose crowd of students. His voice carried, sharp with conviction.

"The law isn't meant to belong to the rich. It's not the playground of silk ties and corporate mergers. It's supposed to be justice – for everyone. If it only protects the powerful, then it's broken."

Some students clapped. Others rolled their eyes. James ran a hand through his hair and shrugged. "That's fine. Disagree. But if you think the system doesn't need fixing, you haven't been paying attention."

Kimberly didn't clap. She just watched. Something about his words stirred a strange feeling – not belief, not quite admiration – but a curiosity that curled somewhere between her ribs. For a moment, she felt like Cosette staring at Marius across a crowded square – idealism and bravado crashing into practicality and patience. She knew better than to fall for theatre. And yet, she stayed, listening. Just a little longer than she meant to. Other students arrived with different kinds of confidence – well-spoken, well-prepared, and sure of their place in the room. Kimberly came from the back of a market truck, but she didn't feel lesser. Just different.

She volunteered for Legal Aid outreach in her first year. It felt familiar – the language of ordinary people, the mess of real problems, the ache for fairness that wasn't always clean or convenient. She listened more than she spoke. But when she spoke, people leaned in.

That was the kind of work Paul Avery would later spend his whole career doing – steady, quiet representation in the courts that rarely made headlines. Kimberly hadn't met him yet, not properly, but even then, she would hear others say: 'Paul did that case,' or 'Paul took that plea.' James talked about justice. Paul lived it.

It wasn't ambition that carried her. It was a sense of purpose. Of balance. Of what was right.

And when her offer came – the winter day she opened the letter confirming her clerkship – she didn't cry. She folded it neatly, put it on the kitchen table, and said, "Nana, we'll need to frame this."

Nana made tea. Kimberly set the table. And the next morning, she was back on the early bus, her collar straight and her heart steady.

The path to law wasn't lightning. It was slow, deliberate and utterly hers.

Paul Avery's path ran parallel – different in texture, but similar in weight. He arrived at Melbourne Law School from Shepparton with a second-hand suitcase and too many expectations. His dorm was cold in winter, hot in summer and always noisy. The heater rattled like it resented being turned on, and the window never quite closed.

He studied late. Not because he liked it, but because he had to. No family firm, no safety net – just a scholarship, a part-time job and a quiet understanding that no one was going to carry him but himself. He didn't speak much in class at first. But he watched. Listened. Took notes in tight, meticulous handwriting. Everything he learned, he earned.

By the second semester, people had started noticing him. Not because he was loud, but because he was consistent. If there was a volunteer list for a legal aid visit, his name was already there. If someone missed a lecture, Paul's notes were the ones they asked for.

He didn't aim for power. He aimed for clarity – and fairness. The law wasn't glamorous. But it mattered. And he was determined to be good at it, not for applause, but because someone in the room needed to be.

His first mock trial was a turning point. He was paired with David Franks, a polished student from Toorak with a wardrobe to match and the confidence of someone who'd grown up around long lunches and silk ties. David was style – Paul was substance.

They both delivered opening arguments. David was slick, full of charm and well-rehearsed phrasing. He sounded like someone already imagining the article that would be written about him one day.

Then Paul stood up.

His speech wasn't theatrical. It didn't dazzle. But it was measured, logical and quietly compelling. He made the case clear – not for the tutor, but for the fictional jury. He didn't just speak. He communicated.

When they finished, the tutor raised an eyebrow and said, "David, that was confident. Paul – that was convincing."

David smiled like he'd won. Paul nodded, quietly satisfied. He wasn't trying to win people over. He was trying to explain the law – and he had.

David didn't bow to his quiet success. He offered Paul a beer that night instead, casually inviting him to join a few others down the road – Xavier boys mostly, laughing too loud, cufflinks still on. It was Paul's first real glimpse of their world. Polished, insular, easy with money and even easier with confidence.

He nursed the beer politely, smiled when expected, and listened more than he spoke. The jokes weren't cruel, but they circled status like a reflex. One of them asked if Paul was clerking yet – Paul hadn't even considered applying.

Paul bought the second round – a stretch for his budget, but he didn't want to stand out. He played the game, laughed at the right moments, and even joined a round of toasts. By the end of it, he was a little drunk, a little dizzy, and quietly surprised by how natural he made it look.

He left not long after, slipping away before a third round could be suggested, walking back to his dorm alone through the warm Melbourne night, replaying the trial in his head. David was good. But Paul had been right.

The Berry Gambit

The Pancake Parlour in Glen Waverley smelled like syrup, whipped butter and nostalgia. The booths were high-backed, the lights dim, the walls cluttered with framed chess trivia and golden mirrors. Near the front, two oversized Mad Hatter chairs flanked a painted chessboard on the floor – part theme, part theatre.

Kimberly liked it. Not because it was stylish, but because it didn't pretend to be anything else.

They took a booth. The waitress barely blinked when Kimberly ordered Earl Grey tea and James ordered a double-shot flat white.

"Tea," James noted. "Didn't peg you for a tea drinker."

Kimberly folded her napkin once. "It's a tea party, isn't it?" she said, nodding toward the chairs. "All that's missing is the Dormouse."

He blinked, then smiled – but she was already reading the menu.

They both ordered the berry stack – hers with extra strawberries, no cream; his with double maple and a side of whipped butter.

When the plates came, Kimberly took a quiet breath before starting – like she did before a moot or cross-checking stock. She pressed a raspberry against her fork, tested the edge of the syrup with a fingertip.

James watched. "You eat like you're assembling a closing argument."

"Pancakes make me happy," she replied, matter-of-factly. "I take them seriously."

He laughed. "That's fair."

They ate without fanfare. The sugar wasn't the point. The calm was.

Afterwards, Kimberly stood and walked over to the chess corner, settling into the white Mad Hatter chair with ease. Her back straight, eyes already scanning the board.

James followed, surprised. "You play?"

She didn't look up. "This isn't a date. It's calibration."

He sat opposite. "You say that like it's less intimate."

"Isn't it?"

They played for forty minutes. She baited. He charged. She sacrificed a pawn without blinking; he overreached. In the end, it was a draw – technical, elegant, unsentimental.

Outside, the evening was soft – warm air, traffic hum, a faint scent of eucalyptus rising from somewhere behind the carpark. James walked with her to his car, keys loose in his hand, still smiling from the chess match.

"You're full of contradictions," he said.

She raised an eyebrow. "Only to people who expect consistency over context."

He laughed, leaned back against the driver's door, fiddling with his keys.

"You want to be kissed," she said calmly.

He blinked. "I – yeah, I do."

She stepped forward, slow and unhurried, until their shoes touched.

"Okay," she said. "But I get to go first."

And then she kissed him – not a brush, not a maybe, but a full, intended, confident kiss. No edge of doubt, no apology. Her hands at his collar. His forgotten entirely.

When it broke, he exhaled like he'd just passed a test he hadn't studied for.

"That's… good," he said.

She nodded. "I know."

And then she got in his car, fastened her seatbelt, and waited for him to catch up.

The Guilded Peel

This chapter spans two worlds: the spectacle of the Melbourne Cup and the performance of the Australian musical premiere. In both, appearances matter – but quiet truths still flicker beneath the surface.

David had asked Paul to join them at the Melbourne Cup – 'It's a big day,' he'd said, brushing a speck of dust from his cuff. 'Everyone who matters will be there. It's not just a show – it's a stage, if you get me.'

Paul wasn't sure what he was walking into. He'd never been to the Melbourne Cup before – never worn a pocket square, never sipped champagne before noon, and never stepped into a world where the colour of your tie meant more than the odds on the race. This wasn't about horses – it was society on display.

James was there, of course. He was always there – part of the gang by inheritance as much as invitation. And beside him stood Kimberly, beautiful and composed, wearing what would later be called the best hat of the day.

It wasn't designer. It wasn't from a boutique. When one of the Brighton girls – one of Allegra's – leaned in and asked who made it, Kimberly simply smiled and said, 'Nana and I.'

James stood near Bronwyn, laughing quietly at something she said – the kind of inside joke that didn't need explaining. But Kimberly's eyes had already found Paul's across the crowd.

And Paul? He met her gaze the way he had at fifteen, beside crates of apples and morning light. For a second, four years vanished. It was the same look – curious, respectful, a little unspoken warmth that neither of them had time for back then.

Now, in polished shoes and borrowed glamour, it passed between them again – not longing, but memory. And it stayed, just long enough to mean something.

Of course, Kimberly was James's girl – that had been clear since the first year. In the world of Xavier boys, lines like that weren't crossed. David hadn't said it about Kimberly, not exactly. He'd said it over lunch once, gesturing vaguely at the group with a glass of wine in hand: 'This is society, mate. There are things you don't do. People you don't surprise. Everyone has their place. And you don't cut in on someone else's story.'

Paul hadn't planned to. But the look didn't ask permission. It just happened – honest, brief, and quietly alive with the past.

Still, the day unfolded easily.

Earlier that week, after the Cup but before the premiere, Bronwyn had received another call from Allegra – just as breezy, just as intentional.

"You've already got tickets, right?" Allegra asked, knowing full well Bronwyn did. "Perfect. You're going with Paul."

"And my aunt?" Bronwyn asked, a soft lilt in her voice, half-laughing.

"Your aunt will understand. Paul Avery looked great in the Birdcage – strong, steady, a little country polish. You two together? Picture perfect. Trust me. He'll clean up well, and you'll look like the most grounded woman in the room."

Bronwyn rolled her eyes. "Ja, well… shouldn't he be the one asking me?" she said, teasing now, her vowels just round enough to hint at her past.

Allegra didn't pause. "Oh no, Bronwyn. We're modern girls. We see what we like – and we go for it."

Bronwyn smiled despite herself.

"You saw how well you two got along at the Cup – come on. He's great. And oh – he's so handsome. That quiet confidence? That's the kind that turns heads without trying."

"Ask him. Say it's your ticket, your idea. Keep it relaxed. He's not going to say no."

And Allegra had been right – about the invitation, about the pairing, about how easy it would feel the moment they stepped into that foyer together.

She found Paul the next day in the university canteen – tray in hand, halfway through a sandwich.

"Hey, Paul," she said, casual but bright. "I've got a spare ticket to the premiere next week. Thought you might like to come with me."

She hesitated – just for a second. Then added, "No pressure, hey? I just thought… we got along well at the Cup."

Paul looked up, a little surprised, then smiled. "Yeah. I'd love to."

Bronwyn's delight was hard to hide – her grin widened as she nodded. "Great. I'll text you the details. Dress code's black tie – but you already wore a pocket square like a pro, so I think you'll be fine."

Not long after the Cup, David was already talking confidently about the upcoming Australian premiere of a major musical. "It's a big night," he said, brushing a speck of dust from his cuff. "Everyone who matters will be there. It's not just a show – it's a stage, if you get me."

Paul chuckled, unsure. "You sound like it's more performance than performance."

David gave him a look – part grin, part sermon. "It is. You reconsidering going?" he asked.

"A little," Paul admitted. "Doesn't feel like my kind of night."

David stopped walking and laid it out like gospel. "You think James is a rebel?" he added, almost laughing. "Please. His father does the legal work for the show. James turns up in a tie that's a little crooked and calls it a protest. But he's there, Paul. He's always there. Because he knows – showing up makes his family look good. That's the rule."

He adjusted his collar and went on. "These nights aren't about comfort. They're about presence. Where you sit, who you speak to, who you show up beside – it all matters. You're being watched, even if you don't see the eyes. Don't try to play someone else's role."

Paul nodded slowly, feeling the weight of it. It wasn't a warning. It wasn't advice. It was a map – the kind that tells you where not to walk.

He didn't reply. But something in his chest tightened – not fear, not defiance. Just the quiet understanding that he'd stepped into someone else's script, and now he had a role to play.

David paused then, voice dropping just enough to feel pointed. "And just so you know – if you don't come, Bronwyn will be devastated and already told Allegra's you're going. This isn't just a plus-one night. It's social currency. The Xavier boys, we show up – we stick to the world. If you pull out now, you don't just let her down. You make all of us look bad."

He tapped Paul lightly on the shoulder as if sealing the moment. "And don't forget – girls don't just want to go to the premiere. They want to show up with the handsome man on their arm. Picture in the Sunday Society Page – that's half the event."

Now here they were, standing in a velvet-lined foyer lit by chandeliers, swapping stories about university mishaps and the strange comfort of pre-show drinks over canapés too small to hold a proper conversation. Allegra, ever gracious and quietly formidable, played her part beside David – not just steering conversations, but shaping them when needed. She softened silences, yes, but she also commanded the room when it mattered.

Kimberly was poised as ever – greeting patrons with soft confidence, chatting lightly with a columnist from the legal review, and excusing herself gracefully when attention turned too close. Her dress was simple but arresting – and that same handmade hat, this time worn with quiet pride, drew more admiration than all the designer labels combined. As Paul entered beside Bronwyn, Kimberly glanced up. Just a flicker – recognition, maybe something else – before she turned back to the conversation at hand. It was only a moment, but it stayed with him longer than it should have. She and Paul spoke a few times – casually, warmly, the way people do when they have no reason not to. Just enough to acknowledge something had once been there. No more than expected. No less than remembered.

At one point, Allegra pulled David gently aside, her eyes following Paul and Bronwyn as they laughed near the curtain. "They're perfect," she said simply. "He softens her. She steadies him. And they look good together – don't pretend you haven't noticed."

David gave a half-smile. "I noticed. I just didn't know you were matchmaking now."

Allegra didn't smile back. "I'm not. I'm just paying attention." She glanced back at Paul and Bronwyn. "He's handsome, you know. A little shy, but the kind of shy that makes people lean in."

David raised an eyebrow.

"Bronwyn's been single too long," Allegra said simply. "And that? That's a match I wouldn't mind saying I had a hand in. Call it a gift."

The six of them gathered later that night at the champagne after-party, still dressed in their finest. Velvet jackets, silk gowns, sharp heels, and tailored cuffs – it felt like stepping into a postcard. David and James held court near the bar while Allegra, Bronwyn, and Kimberly clustered near the edge of the terrace, glasses of Moët in hand. Paul drifted between them, laughing easily, more comfortable than he'd expected to be.

There was a moment – brief, electric – when a photographer angled his lens toward Bronwyn and Paul as they stood beside the grand piano, drinks in hand. The next morning's paper caught it perfectly.

"Who is the handsome stranger by Bronwyn Westwood's side?"

The society editor, of course, knew exactly who Bronwyn was – Brighton's own, a staple of quiet appearances, always present but never in bold. But Paul? Paul was a mystery. Not Toorak, not Xavier, not mentioned at any luncheon or preview. Not yet. And that made him more interesting.

The editor circled his name in red, scribbled a note in the margin: Find out who he is.

Allegra beamed when she saw it over brunch. Sitting with the girls in a café that spilt onto the Brighton footpath, she folded the paper neatly and tapped the page with one perfectly manicured nail.

"I told you," she said, lifting her coffee. "Perfect match."

Kimberly glanced down at the photo, her smile calm, composed. Bronwyn blushed and said nothing – but her hand lingered for a moment on the page, as if trying to hold it in place a little longer.

The Flannel Fig

Bronwyn curled her legs beneath her on Paul's narrow dorm bed, the sheets slightly crinkled from earlier study. His room was small, warm, and faintly smelled of eucalyptus shampoo and old carpet. A fan hummed near the window. She liked the stillness here – no music, no chaos. Just them.

Paul sat on the floor, back against the wall, flipping through a casebook with half-interest. He looked up when she exhaled sharply through her nose.

"What?" he asked.

She smiled. "Eish, Paul – your handwriting is something else. Totally unreadable."

He held up the notebook in protest. "That's how farmers write legislation."

Bronwyn laughed – real and soft – and leaned over the edge of the bed to kiss his temple. "Ja, well… you're not just a farmer."

He looked up at her, that slow, steady look of his. "And you're not just Brighton."

Later, Bronwyn sat barefoot in one of Paul's old flannel shirts, flipping through a textbook she wasn't really reading. Paul leaned beside her, one hand resting on the edge of the mattress, the other close to hers, but not quite touching.

"It's nice here, hey," she said softly. "So quiet."

"Especially with you," he replied.

She looked over at him. He met her eyes – steady, soft.

He reached for her hand. She didn't move.

And then, slowly, carefully, she leaned in – not like she was falling, but like she was choosing.

The kiss wasn't urgent. It deepened because it felt safe to do so. When she slipped the shirt off, he paused – just for a second – to ask with his eyes if she was sure.

She nodded once.

And that was enough.

They moved carefully, as if they didn't want to break the moment. No fireworks, no declarations. Just touch, trust and something warmer than either had expected.

Afterwards, Bronwyn lay with her back to him, his arm draped loosely around her waist. She traced circles on his forearm with her fingertip – quiet and calm.

"I feel like myself here," she murmured. "Like… properly myself."

Paul kissed the back of her shoulder. "Good."

First Pick

Kimberly parked behind the loading bay, the Hilux already backed in, its tray half empty.

Angelo had made the run, just like her dad had taught him – engine warm by four, paperwork in the cab, ABC News on low. A stockhand through and through – and a good one. Her father liked him. Reliable. Strong. Quiet. But not a buyer.

As Kimberly stepped out of the car, ledger under one arm, belt clip secured with two thousand dollars in neat fifties, Angelo gave her a small nod.

"Good morning, Kimberly," he said – voice solid, respectful, not stiff. Just a real hello.

"Oh, good morning, Angelo," she replied warmly. "How's your beautiful wife?"

He smiled, just a flicker.

"Still putting up with me."

"Saintly woman," Kimberly said, deadpan, already walking.

He chuckled softly.

He didn't follow her in – too many of the boys from the stalls were having their early smoke outside the gates.

Angelo joined them for the daily routine, but when the time came, he'd load whatever she bought, no questions asked – same as always.

Her dad was on holiday – finally. He'd taken the caravan up to Mildura with Mum, spending a couple of weeks on the Murray. No phone. No freight orders. Just the sun and free time.

Back at the shop, two of the regulars – Luca and Donna – could handle the front counter and prep work. But someone still had to buy. Someone who knew the rhythms, the prices, the way her father always made the calls. That someone was Kimberly.

She didn't argue. She just packed the ledger.

Inside, the market buzzed like a machine running on low oil – noise, cold air, forklifts beeping, fruit boxes stacked shoulder-high. The floor smelled like wet cardboard and oranges.

Kimberly moved with intent. She wasn't wandering. This wasn't a family outing.

The air inside Stall One was sharp with citrus and chill. Plastic crates lined the benches, all morning-silent and waiting to be picked over. Most stallhands were still dragging pallets from the cool room, but the man behind the display – broad-shouldered, in a faded grey hoodie – was already arranging rows of lemons by size.

Kimberly recognised him instantly – even from behind.

The way he stood – deliberate, patient – and the curl of his fingers around the edge of a box. She didn't hesitate.

"Good morning, Paul," she said, warm as ever – her proper voice, the one that greeted magistrates and receptionists and deli managers alike. She put just enough music in it to make it hers. Kind. Clear. Unmistakable.

He turned around like he'd heard a melody, not a name.

"Kimberly," he said, surprised – but with a smile already forming. He straightened up from behind a stack of punnets, wiping his hands on a towel that had seen better days.

"Didn't expect you."

"Likewise." Her eyes flicked to the branded apron he wore.

"You're actually working the stall?"

"Couple of mornings a week," he said easily. "Helps keep me awake for constitutional law."

She tilted her head. "I thought your family owned half the valley."

He gave a modest shrug. "Avery Orchards is still an orchard. Fruit doesn't move itself."

A pause. Then, lightly:

"Dad reckons if I want to keep the surname, I should know what a four a.m. start feels like."

Kimberly looked at him properly now – sleeves rolled, boots stained, clipboard tucked under one arm. No entourage. No special treatment.

"You've been here since two?"

"Yeah." He yawned, openly this time. "Read till midnight, quick sleep, straight in."

He looked faintly embarrassed. "It's not as noble as it sounds. I like it. You know how the place gets – noise, forklifts, bad coffee. Clears my head."

She smiled despite herself. "I'll take your word for it."

He grinned, rubbing a palm over his face. "Still, seeing you here might be the only thing keeping me upright at this point."

She laughed – not loudly, but enough for him to hear. The sound hung between them, light and fleeting.

"So… how's Bronwyn going?" she asked, a little too lightly – the way someone asks a question they already know the answer to. Allegra had already filled her in.

Paul grinned, not missing the game.

"She's doing well. We had dinner at her parents' place last week."

He chuckled. "Kimberly, their garage is bigger than Dad's whole Harvest shed."

Kimberly raised her eyebrows. “Oh gosh.”

Paul nodded. “And dinner – they called it *Karoo lamb*. Spicy, tender, nothing like the roasts I grew up with. This one came with a story and three kinds of side dishes.”

He laughed, but there was genuine appreciation in his voice.

He paused for a second, then added more softly,

“I want to take Bronwyn to the farm next month. Show her the Pink Ladies just before the pick – when they blush up red and cling to the branches like they don’t want to go.”

His voice dipped with something close to wonder.

“She should see that. Also… Mum and Dad would love to meet her.”

Kimberly went to dinner at James’s parents’ house was catered – for just the four of them. A private chef, linen napkins, three courses announced like headlines. It was quiet, polished and not one dish came with seconds.

James had come to her place once for a Sunday roast. Her dad carved the meat, her mum passed the peas, and Nana brought out a sponge cake still warm from the tin, dusted with icing sugar and pride.

She let out a short laugh.

“Yeah… we both knew which one tasted better.”

“Well. Let’s get you through it, then.”

Without hesitation, she stepped toward the ledger clipped to the crate stack, flipping through it with practised fingers.

“Okay, Paul. Work time.”

She scanned the morning allocations, brow furrowing slightly in thought.

“Two trays of white nectarines from Booth’s,” she said, more to herself than to anyone in particular. “One box of Shepard avocados. Five bunches of silverbeet, if they’re not limp. And—”

She looked up sharply, eyes meeting his.

"Did your lot bring the pink grapefruit today?"

He blinked, then smiled. "Yeah. Dad's trialling a smaller run this season – limited crates. Want me to check if there's any left?"

"Check?" Her tone was amused. "Paul, if you've got them, you're giving me two. Non-negotiable."

He laughed, holding up both hands in surrender. "All right, all right. You're as bad as my aunt."

"Worse," she said, turning back to the clipboard. "I write things down."

She paused as they reached the apples. Her eyes scanned the label: *Avery Orchards – Pink Lady*.

"Pink Ladies?" she said. "It's too early – they'd still be sharp unless you've—"

She stopped herself. Looked at Paul.

"Picked a test block early," he said, already reaching down. "Avery's running a new CA program – dropped the temp, let them mellow in storage. Took the bite off without losing crunch."

Without another word, he plucked one from the top row – a perfect apple, blushed deep pink, skin unblemished. He turned back to her, holding it out with a soft but deliberate smile.

"Please," he said. "Try it."

She looked at him just for a beat – half amused, half curious – then took the apple without flinching. Not performative, not coy. Just confident.

She bit into it.

Crunch. Juicy. Sweet, but still holding that early-season zing.

She blinked. "Okay," she said around the bite. "That's… annoyingly good."

Kimberly smiled again, wiping her fingers on a paper towel from her coat pocket, already moving onto the next order. Professional. Efficient. But now, with half an apple in her hand.

And Paul, trailing behind slightly, watching her do what she does best.

"They're good," she said, "but it's still early season. I'll take five trays, but I'm not paying more than twenty-two a tray."

Paul raised an eyebrow. "You drive a hard bargain."

She didn't blink. "That's what Dad pays when they're perfect. These are close, but not singing yet."

He gave a little shrug, fighting back a grin. "Anything for Ms Doors."

That earned a glance. Half a smile.

"You remember that?" she asked.

"Hard to forget someone who knows how to negotiate peach prices and out-argue a Constitutional Law tutor in the same breath."

She didn't answer right away. Just jotted the price in her ledger, calm and in control. But the edge of her mouth curved slightly, as if letting herself enjoy it for a second.

Behind them, Angelo reappeared with the trolley.

"I've got the trays," he said, ready to load.

Kimberly handed him the slip. "Add these to the nectarines."

Paul nodded toward her car. "You want a hand getting it all packed?"

She shook her head. "I've got it."

"Of course you do."

She met his eyes then – not long, but long enough to say thank you without saying it aloud.

Then she was already moving, ledger tucked under her arm, pencil behind her ear, half an apple in her hand.

Paul's boss approached. "Professor," he said, mock-formal. "You mind checking the cool room? The aircon's making that noise again – sounds like a mower chewing up gravel."

Paul gave a quick salute. "On it."

As he turned to go, he glanced back at Kimberly, half-grinning.

"She drives a hard bargain," he said, loud enough for his boss to hear.

As Paul disappeared into the back of the stall, Kimberly called after his boss, casually but with genuine interest.

"You hired Paul?"

The man chuckled, not stopping. "Interviewed him when he was five."

Kimberly raised an eyebrow.

He turned halfway, walking backwards now, his grin wide. "How can anyone say no to an Avery boy?"

Then he was gone – clipboard bobbing, voice already calling to someone about pallets near the back ramp.

Kimberly stood still for a moment, pencil hovering. Her eyes drifted toward the cool room, where Paul had disappeared into shadows and cold air.

The strawberries were tight that week – late-season, deep red, and in short supply. Kimberly stood at the stall, clipboard in hand, eyeing the neat stacks of trays behind the vendor.

"Ten trays," she said to another vendor.

The man crossed his arms. "That's most of what I've got left. Two thirty-nine the lot."

She gave a slight nod, as if calculating. "On account?"

"If you want them held, sure. But at that price, they'll be gone in half an hour."

Kimberly paused, then tapped her clipboard with one finger. "Two hundred. Cash. Right now."

He looked up, surprised. "Two hundred?"

"No delays. No haggling. No paperwork. Just clean cash and I'm gone."

The vendor scratched his chin. He looked past her at the growing line of buyers, then back at her – the bag at her hip already unzipped.

"You always that quick?"

"Only when it counts," she said, peeling off four fifties.

He grinned, took the notes and waved toward the stack. "You're your father's daughter, no doubt about it."

She offered a quiet smile. "And his accountant."

The orders were done. The ledger closed. Angelo had already pulled the Hilux around to the front, stacked and secured. Kimberly slipped the pencil behind her ear and unclipped the cash pouch from her belt, locking it back into her shoulder bag.

She allowed herself a small moment of calm – just one – and walked to the market canteen.

Tea. Hot, strong, plain. The kind that cleared your head more than it woke you up.

She sat at a scratched metal table near the wall, cradling the paper cup between both hands. The market's noise was still humming behind the glass – forklifts, voices, crates landing hard – but here, it was quieter. Slower.

Across the room, Paul sat with a coffee. Same table as always. His high-vis vest slung over the back of the chair, hood still damp with early morning mist. He glanced at his watch.

"Seven," he said aloud, like confirming it for himself. Then again, to her:

"Okay. That's me. Finish work. Back to uni."

He stood and stretched, a bit stiff from the cold.

"Shower. Shave. I'll just make it for the ten a.m. Torts class."

Paul blew across the rim of his coffee, then glanced back over at her.

"We're doing *Donoghue v Stevenson* today," he said, half-grinning. "Snail in the bottle. Torts classic."

Kimberly didn't even blink. "Have you looked at *Grant v Australian Knitting Mills*?"

He paused, caught off guard. "Is that the one with the underpants?"

"Woollen ones. Dermatitis. South Australia. It sharpens the duty of care argument."

She sipped her tea like it was nothing.

Paul nodded slowly, impressed. "You've already read ahead?"

"I don't have time not to."

There was no brag in it. Just a fact. A schedule packed so tightly it didn't allow for catching up later.

Paul leaned back in his chair, coffee half-finished. "Should've known you'd already be two weeks ahead."

"You should read it before class," she added. "Professor Lang loves using it to ambush people."

Closing Beat.

She walked the long way around to the flower stall.

It wasn't in the budget – not really – but the orders had been strong this morning. Prices held. Margins good. She'd kept the costs tight, picked every crate with care.

She always did.

Only once she'd finished – once the fruit and veg were bought, the numbers made sense, the truck was packed – then she allowed herself to think it.

What if.

She handed over two hundred dollars for a mix of autumn blooms – wild marigolds, rust-coloured tulips, cabbage roses that looked like spun silk.

For the footpath.

For anyone walking past who needed to see something living and sudden and full of colour.

Kimberly Doors always did the work first.

Then, if there was enough left – she bought the *what if.*

She stepped into the noise and chill of the market, hair back, coat zipped, breath rising in thin clouds.

The belt pouch rested neatly on her hip – clipped tight, worn smooth, familiar.

Inside: two thousand dollars in cash.

Not a round number for show.

A working number.

It was what her father carried on a solid buying day. Enough to stock the shop, buy quality, and still hold margin.

Cash worked here.

Cash spoke.

The stallholders knew the Doors – and they knew Kimberly.

She wasn't tagging along anymore.

She was buying.

Back at the shop, Angelo was already unloading the Hilux. Kimberly joined him without a word, stacking crates in rhythm. The Pink Ladies went straight to the front shelf – no cool room. Early, but ready.

She wiped the timber clean, reached for the chalkboard, and wrote:

Early Pick Pink Ladies

Small run. Great flavour. Still a touch of zing.

We're backing them.

She clipped it in place, then unwrapped the flowers – marigolds, tulips and cabbage roses soft as silk – and arranged them in buckets by the footpath. Bold colour. Clean angles. Something to make people stop. A gesture, not a decoration.

By twelve thirty, she was changed and back in the car. Monash was only minutes away. She parked behind the law building and headed straight to her one p.m. lecture.

Not *Donoghue v Stevenson* – that had been Paul's morning.

Kimberly's class was quieter, heavier – case law without charm, just structure and consequence. The kind that sorted the ambitious from the easily distracted. She'd read ahead, annotated twice, and walked in knowing the key rulings before the lecturer reached the second slide.

She made one clean point when called on – not to impress, just to keep pace with herself. Then she took notes like someone who couldn't afford to miss a thing.

By the time it ended, she was already thinking about dinner.

She was home by five.

Lemon chicken went into the oven alongside sweet potatoes and carrots she'd peeled the night before. Nana was knitting at the table, eyes flicking up over her glasses when Kimberly came in.

"Busy day?"

Kimberly set down the grocery bag. "Margins held. Flowers were extra. I paid cash."

"That's how your father did it."

Dinner was simple and warm. They ate slowly, without noise. Two women who didn't need to fill the silence to enjoy the company.

"Feels like a proper girls' night," Nana said.

Kimberly smiled. "The original kind."

After the dishes were done and Nana settled in front of the evening news, Kimberly brewed chamomile, sat on her bed with her notebook open, and reviewed her readings for the next day.

No catching up. No letting things slide.

There was no one else keeping her on track.

Just her.

The day was done.

The ledger balanced.

The house was still.

And Kimberly Doors – daughter, law student, fruit buyer – was ready for tomorrow.

Midnight Margin

The best fruit hangs closest to overripe.

The best moments – just before they pass.

That's where the margin lives. Midnight, sugar, silence – and what comes next.

The fruit basket was simple, elegant – ripe peaches, blood plums, firm nectarines and Avery Orchard apricots, with a scattering of tiny green figs nestled among dark leaves. Kimberly had picked them herself that morning, just after opening the shutters of her parents' shop in Mulgrave.

Later, in the quiet of the house, she wrapped the basket in clear cellophane, smoothing the edges with care, and tied it closed with a length of ribbon she found in Nana's old sewing tin.

Back on the farm, Paul was getting ready to leave after Christmas when his mother pressed a brown paper bag into his hands. Inside were a few jars of homemade jam, still warm from the morning sun.

"Mum… this is homemade jam. You think fancy people want plum jam?"

She gave him a wink. "Paul Avery, do you know how nice toast is with good plum jam? They'll love it. Trust me."

David did what he did best – placed a few strategic phone calls. Premium champagne and wine from a boutique winery in Red Hill arrived later that afternoon, chilled, wrapped and perfectly labelled, as though the bottles themselves knew they were meant to be admired.

Bronwyn had stopped by a florist on Church Street and selected a spray of seasonal flowers – soft whites, blush pinks and eucalyptus green – to dress the house and the long dinner table. The arrangement arrived in the early evening, the scent of jasmine and garden roses drifting gently through the holiday home as if summer had been invited inside.

James brought nothing. He arrived late, dressed impeccably, and kissed everyone on the cheek as if his presence were a contribution enough. No one mentioned it – not directly – but Allegra raised an eyebrow behind her champagne flute, and Kimberly, arranging her fruit basket on the sideboard, said nothing at all.

Now Allegra arrived an hour before the others, her car loaded with carefully packed takeaway boxes from the famous Altona restaurant – each container labelled in delicate handwriting, some still faintly warm.

She had picked up the order herself, arriving at the back kitchen door just as the chef was finishing the final flourish on the cheesecake – a cool crown of Chantilly cream shaped into soft peaks.

The chef had wiped his hands and stepped forward with quiet pride.

"This should be served just slightly chilled – not fridge-cold. Let it breathe for twenty minutes first."

Allegra nodded, listening carefully as he laid out the reheating instructions for the duck confit and the squash blossom tarts. She could have brushed it off – could have claimed to know – but she didn't. She stood there, elegant in linen and sunglasses, nodding seriously, committing each step to memory.

"I'll follow it to the letter," she promised. "You've trusted me with a masterpiece. I won't ruin it with a microwave."

The chef smiled, pleased, and packed the final container with slow, ceremonial care.

Now, in the Point Nepean kitchen, Allegra moved swiftly but precisely – peeling back the cellophane, setting ceramic trays on the bench, mentally rehearsing her timeline. She lined the oven shelves with foil. She decanted sauces into delicate bowls. She placed the cheesecake in the fridge – but not too deep – and set a reminder on her phone to take it out in time.

By nine o'clock, the night had settled into its rhythm – music low, wine flowing, warm laughter echoing across the patio. The patio heater cast a soft golden halo, and someone had brought out a speaker that drifted between Ella Fitzgerald and modern covers of love songs.

James and Kimberly curled into one another on the lounge chairs near the balcony – her head against his chest, his fingers absentmindedly tracing hers. They didn't talk much. They didn't need to.

David and Allegra stood arm-in-arm by the outdoor bar, sharing quiet jokes, clinking glasses in a rhythm that felt like second nature. She looked radiant in the soft lighting – all poise and polish – but with just enough vulnerability in her eyes to suggest she still cared if he looked at her a certain way.

Bronwyn and Paul were seated side by side at the edge of the long dining table, their knees barely brushing. She was laughing – lightly, politely – at something someone across the table said, but her hand never reached for his. And his eyes wandered more than they rested.

They looked like a couple. They arrived as a couple. But something in the air around them felt… staged. As if they were sharing a scene, not a moment.

Allegra noticed.

From across the patio, she sipped her wine and watched – not with malice, not quite – but with the quiet attentiveness of someone who had spent her whole life reading people the way others read menus.

"They're not quite right," she murmured to David, almost absently.

He followed her gaze and didn't pretend not to see it.

"Maybe they're still finding their rhythm," he offered.

Allegra didn't answer. Her expression softened – just a little – but the calculation in her eyes never fully left.

"They're beautiful together," she said finally. "But beauty's not always enough."

Then she turned away, already thinking of the next move.

The cheesecake was flawless – creamy, dense, piped with Chantilly like someone had used a ruler. A centrepiece, glossy and proud.

Allegra – opened the jar without fuss. A spoonful of plum jam, deep and dark, landed softly on the plate.

It wasn't meant to be a big thing. But then someone took a bite.

Silence. Then:

"Oh."

Another bite. Then laughter. "That's… that's ridiculous."

Even David Franks, watching from the other side of the patio heater, raised an eyebrow.

"It makes it ten times better," someone said. "Where did you get this?"

Paul, half-smiling, shrugged.

"Mum packed it. Said plum jam goes with everything. Especially toast."

He paused. Then added, "Guess she was right."

Allegra, still chewing, nodded. "She was very, very right."

"Right," she said, eyes sparkling. "Let's hear from my legal friends – what are going to be the great legal adventures this summer?"

Internship List

Kimberly took a slow sip, then replied evenly, "Kiriakopoulos & Anagnostou. Probate law. Oakleigh."

Paul blinked. "That's not a law firm – that's a Scrabble championship."

Bronwyn narrowed her eyes. "Say that again?"

Kimberly smiled, poised. "Ki-ree-ah-KO-po-lous. And Ah-nag-NOS-too."

James leaned back. "Bless you."

The table laughed.

Allegra grinned. "That sounds like a monastery and a mezzé platter."

"They're brilliant," Kimberly added, unfazed. "Mr Kiriakopoulos can quote the Wills Act and your grandmother's baking method in the same breath."

David raised a brow. "And you can actually say their names?"

"I practised," Kimberly said. "I wasn't going to call my supervising solicitor Mr Alphabet."

Allegra swirled her wine, turning to Paul with a smile that was almost too casual.

"And what about you, Paul?" she asked. "What corner of the legal empire did you find yourself in?"

He wiped his hands on a linen napkin, glanced briefly at Bronwyn, then back to his glass.

"Footscray," he said. "Small firm. One lawyer, one receptionist, a kettle that whistles when it's ready."

Laughter flickered around the table – gently, this time.

"Mostly Magistrates' Court," he continued. "Drink driving. A few probate matters. A lot of wills."

David leaned in, half curious. "Wills? That sounds… quiet."

Paul shrugged. "Sometimes. Unless the family's already fighting. Then it's just grief with paperwork."

There was a pause. Not heavy – just honest.

Kimberly gave him a thoughtful nod. "That's still real law. Families, consequences. Things that last."

Paul smiled faintly. "I like it. You meet people on their ordinary days, not just the dramatic ones."

Bronwyn said nothing, sipping her wine too quickly.

Allegra tilted her head, her tone warm but unreadable. "That's very you, Paul."

He looked up at her. "What does that mean?"

She smiled but didn't answer. Instead, she turned and reached for the dessert plates, shifting the mood before anyone could press further.

As the teasing around Paul's Footscray exploits began to fade, Allegra turned, grinning.

"All right then – let's hear from the prince of pride himself. James?"

James lifted his glass like it was part of a coronation.

"Brady and Sanderson," he said smoothly. "Naturally."

Bronwyn rolled her eyes affectionately. "Of course."

David smirked. "Was there ever any doubt?"

Paul raised a brow. "So… what was your role, officially? Chief Polo Shirt Consultant?"

"Close," James replied, unbothered. "They let me write a memo. Once. Then I spent a week shadowing my dad through six boardrooms and three golf lunches."

"Exhausting," Allegra deadpanned.

Kimberly leaned forward, sweetly. "Did you at least get a firm pen?"

"I got a Montblanc and a car space," James said. "And a standing lunch order from the RACV Club."

Everyone laughed, though a few glances were exchanged – the kind that weighed the difference between earned and inherited.

"But hey," James added, flashing that signature grin, "the perks are nice. And someone's got to inherit the paperwork."

Paul took a slow sip of wine, smiling faintly. "Sure. Just don't forget how to find your own kettle."

As the laughter around James's golf lunches subsided, Allegra clinked her spoon gently against her glass again.

"And finally," she said with mock ceremony, "the man of mystery, the crown prince of legal pedigree – Mr David Franks. Where did you deign to summer?"

David placed his fork down like he was stepping onto a stage.

"Franks & Valentine," he said, drawing out the name with just the right blend of self-awareness and inherited entitlement. "Chancery floor. Crystal water jug. Two secretaries and one terrified junior assigned to fetch me coffee."

Kimberly grinned. "So the usual, then?"

Paul chuckled. "Do they even let you touch real files?"

"Oh no," David replied. "They're afraid I might stain the letterhead."

James leaned back, arms folded. "Let's be honest. They're just polishing the plaque for your door."

David shrugged, deadpan. "They already put the tag up: David Franks – Future Partner, Group & Private Wealth Division. Nice font."

Bronwyn raised an eyebrow. "Isn't your family, like… half their client list?"

David smiled. "Three-quarters. But who's counting?"

The table groaned and laughed.

Allegra rested a hand on his arm, shaking her head. "You're awful," she said fondly.

"And punctual," he added. "My biggest achievement this summer was learning how not to roll my eyes during asset protection briefings."

Paul raised his glass. "To inherited glory."

David clinked back. "And inherited headaches."

Allegra gave a playful shrug, then added with a glint in her eye, "Honestly, I feel sorry for most of you, schlepping your way through the summer."

She swept her gaze around the table with mock sympathy. "Bronwyn and I" – she tipped her head toward her friend – "are going to Byron Bay… followed by Club Med in Bali." She winked at Bronwyn.

Bronwyn clinked her glass against Allegra's. "Much better training for life, hey?"

Laughter broke out again – lighter this time, tinged with longing, like the sound of waves just out of reach.

Allegra stood by the patio doorway, half-shadowed by the soft flicker of fairy lights. The music had dipped to a low hum now – something jazzy and slow – and the night was curling into its final act.

She watched her friends – laughing, stretched out across lounge chairs, barefoot and wine-loose, glowing in that in-between hour where everything felt possible.

A breeze stirred, scented faintly with sea salt and lemon eucalyptus. And just like that, she was back beneath the jacaranda trees at Mentone Girls' Grammar, the summer sun splintering through lavender blossoms and casting dappled shadows on manicured lawns. In their crisp red blazers and straw hats, the Year 8 students moved in clusters, laughter and chatter trailing behind them like perfume.

Allegra had lingered near one of those trees, watching the new girl – Bronwyn – who sat alone on a bench, her posture composed but her eyes scanning the unfamiliar grounds. Her South African accent had already drawn whispers and sideways glances from some of the other girls.

Allegra approached, her steps measured and calm.

"Mind if I sit?" she'd asked.

Bronwyn looked up, a flicker of surprise in her eyes. "Sure."

They sat in silence for a moment, the distant hum of cicadas filling the space.

"I like your accent," Allegra said finally.

Bronwyn's lips curved into a small, cautious smile. "Thanks. Not everyone does."

Allegra shrugged. "Well, not everyone has taste."

Bronwyn chuckled, the tension easing from her shoulders.

It was quiet, almost unremarkable – and yet, that moment mattered. A bond had formed. Not through grand gestures, but through stillness, kindness and the rare ease of being seen.

Back on the balcony, Allegra's gaze found Bronwyn among the group – her laughter as warm and genuine as it had been all those years ago. A smile touched Allegra's lips. Their friendship had weathered the tests of time, distance and life's quiet reckonings.

She raised her glass slightly in Bronwyn's direction – a silent toast to the girl who had once sat alone beneath a jacaranda tree, and to the enduring bond that had grown from that simple hello.

People often mistook her – thought she was cold, curated, maybe even a little cruel. But they didn't know how much she loved this – loved *them.* Loved the feel of the night coming together, the table set just right, the view they would remember.

She glanced toward Kimberly – radiant in that red dress, laughing now with James. But what Allegra noticed most, *truly* noticed, was how Kimberly had spoken earlier to the bakery shop assistant during pickup – not just polite, but *equal*. The same tone she'd use for a king or a stranger on the tram.

Allegra envied that. She couldn't do it – not like that. Her charm was polished, not effortless. Her warmth wore heels.

And that was fine.

She turned back to the night, letting the moment settle around her like silk. She didn't want the world to guess her choices. She wanted to make them herself. People talked about modern women as if it meant rejecting tradition – as if ambition and softness couldn't exist in the same heart.

But Allegra *wanted* to marry David. Fully. Freely. She wanted children. A home. Long tables, clinking glasses, the sounds of joy she had curated – not because someone told her to, but because it made her heart sing.

It wasn't surrender.

It was design.

And if that didn't fit someone else's script for what a modern woman should be – well, that was *their* limitation, not hers.

The music changed just after eleven thirty – someone had queued up a playlist with real rhythm now: Motown, old soul, shimmering pop from the early 1980s. The fairy lights twinkled a little brighter, the champagne flutes stayed full, and the terrace had turned into a dance floor without anyone really planning it.

David spun Allegra once, her silk dress catching the air like a sail. Bronwyn danced with Kimberly for a song or two, both of them laughing harder than they had in weeks. Even Paul had been pulled up by James – who, half-sloshed and overly confident, tried to teach him the two-step and promptly tripped over the outdoor rug.

Everyone was a little flushed, a little tipsy, glowing in the way people do when the year is nearly over and everything still feels possible.

Then the music dipped into something slower – something warm and golden, like liquid brass. Sam Cooke, maybe. Or Otis Redding.

Kimberly stood near the balcony rail, her hair pinned high, that stunning red dress hugging her like a whisper. She looked out at the night for a moment – then turned back, her eyes finding James across the patio.

She smiled – slow, knowing – and raised her hand.

"Come here," she said, her voice low but impossible to ignore. "Kiss me."

James didn't speak. Didn't smirk. He just moved – cutting across the fairy lights and candle shadows toward her like he was answering a call older than words.

They met in the centre of the patio, laughter and music spinning around them. She placed her hands on his collar; his fingers found her waist – and then they kissed.

Properly. Fully. With the ease of people who had fought, forgiven, and remembered exactly why it mattered.

Someone whistled. Allegra clapped.

Bronwyn looked away, just slightly.

And Paul? He watched for a second too long, then turned toward the bar, pouring another glass.

The countdown hadn't begun yet – but the night was already beginning to turn.

As midnight drew closer, a gentle hush began to fall over the group. The last song faded into a background rhythm, and couples gathered instinctively near the balcony rail.

The night was warm, the breeze soft off the bay. Champagne glasses clinked quietly as hands found hands, and for a few minutes, no one spoke much at all.

Then, just as the clock struck twelve, the first explosion lit up the sky.

From their position on the balcony – high above Point Nepean, facing the water – they had a view few Melburnians ever knew existed: the entire bay lit up like a circuit board, fireworks arcing from every corner.

To the east, the city skyline shimmered like a mirage, glowing and pulsing in technicolour. Docklands, St Kilda, the Yarra – even hints of Dandenong light – the whole basin blinked and boomed with celebration.

"Oh my God," Bronwyn breathed. "You can see the whole thing."

David grinned. "This is insane."

Allegra stood apart for a moment, one hand resting lightly on the glass balustrade, the other cradling her champagne. Her hair shimmered in the light of the explosions, but her face was still – not sad, not smug. Just… still.

Kimberly turned to her. "This is why you picked here."

Allegra nodded once. "It's Melbourne's best-kept secret. The whole city puts on a show – you just have to know where to stand."

James let out a long, low whistle. "And you rented this place for the week, for us to stay one night?"

"Worth every cent," Allegra said, eyes still on the horizon.

Paul stepped up beside her, watching the light dance on the water.

"You always did know how to stage an ending."

Allegra smiled but didn't look at him.

"It's not about the ending, Paul. It's about what people remember."

The sky bloomed again in bursts of gold and violet. Fireworks echoed like distant applause.

All around them – laughter and kisses, arms wrapped around waists, hands laced tightly together.

Paul and Bronwyn kissed – politely. Carefully. The kind of kiss you give when you know others are watching.

Kimberly and James didn't come up for air.

Allegra turned toward David and embraced him – proud, radiant, knowing. This was her beloved, her future husband, and in that moment, she felt the beauty of it settle in her bones.

As the last of the fireworks faded and the champagne dulled to warmth, the laughter softened. The couples drifted back inside two by two – arms around waists, heels dangling from fingertips, silk dresses catching in the breeze.

A Different Orchard

After the summer internships wrapped up, Paul returned early to university. There was only a short break before the academic year officially began – maybe two weeks – and he didn't see much point in going back to Shepparton just for that. Instead, he used the time to catch up on schoolwork and get a head start on the semester.

David, longing for a change of pace – even a brief one – joined Allegra and Bronwyn in Bali for a quick holiday. He needed the sun, the distraction, and, more than he liked to admit, he missed Allegra.

Paul's life soon slipped back into the cadence of study. One late afternoon, after a long session in the university library gathering photocopies and nursing a lukewarm Coke, Paul balanced the messy stack of papers in one arm and headed out, squinting against the low sun.

At the cafeteria, he grabbed a sandwich, exchanging the usual smiles with the staff. Paul was always polite, always with that easy-going grin that made people feel seen without making a show of it.

It was there he noticed Helena.

She worked the counter some afternoons – a bright, quick laugh and a Datsun 200B parked haphazardly near the side fence. Paul had always greeted her with the same warm smile he offered everyone, but today she stood outside by her car, frustration written plainly across her face.

The Datsun coughed and spluttered but refused to start.

Paul approached, setting his sandwich and Coke on the hood.

"Need a hand?" he asked, already rolling up his sleeves.

Helena looked up, cheeks flushed. "It's dead. Again."

She pulled out her phone, ready to call her brother for help.

Paul shook his head lightly, lifting the hood himself. "Mind if I have a look?"

Helena hesitated, surprised, but stepped aside gratefully.

Paul fiddled under the hood for a few moments, his movements confident and sure.

"Try it now," he said, leaning back from the engine.

The Datsun roared to reluctant life.

Helena's face lit up, part surprise, part delight.

"You're a magician," she laughed.

Paul chuckled, brushing his hands against his jeans. "Just stubborn. Like your Datsun."

She looked at him, wide-eyed. "How did you know what to do?"

He shrugged modestly. "Country boy. Been fixing old cars since I was tall enough to hold a wrench. If it's got an engine, I've probably patched it up at least once."

They stood there a moment longer, the soft hum of the engine between them. The attraction was immediate, warm and easy – like slipping into a conversation halfway through.

Helena grinned. "My brother's usually the one rescuing me. He'll be impressed. Family cars always break down at the worst times."

Paul laughed. "You're not wrong. I grew up around fruit farms – old utes, dusty tractors, the occasional lemon of a Datsun. Fixing engines was survival."

"And now law?" she teased, curiosity sparking in her voice.

"Fruit and law," Paul said, smiling easily. "That's my odd little combination."

They talked without effort, words flowing as naturally as the late afternoon light stretching across the parking lot. No need for pretence, no careful performances. Just two people, finding common ground without even trying.

One gesture at a time, Paul was finding his way back.

It started simply.

One night after her shift, Helena leaned casually against her Datsun, tossing her keys from hand to hand, her smile easy and expectant.

"Coffee?" she asked. "Or maybe something stronger?"

Paul hesitated for the briefest moment, guilt nipping at the edges of his mind. Bronwyn was still a part of his life – but that life had been unravelling, thread by thread, for months. He hadn't meant for this to happen. He hadn't been looking.

But the truth was undeniable: he liked Helena too much to pretend he didn't feel it.

He smiled – small and resigned – and nodded.

They found a little diner tucked away behind the university – sticky booths, chipped mugs, the smell of coffee and old vinyl records. They talked about everything and nothing: family stories, terrible first cars, the absurdities of growing up between dusty farms and dusty textbooks.

Helena laughed easily, genuinely. Paul felt lighter around her, less guarded.

When they finally wandered back to the car, the night was heavy with the scent of damp grass and the distant salt of the bay.

They stood for a moment by the Datsun, neither quite willing to say goodnight.

Paul opened the passenger door for her, teasing. "Need a driver in case she doesn't start again?"

Helena grinned, stepping closer.

Without thinking, without ceremony, he leaned in.

Their lips met – not awkwardly, not hesitantly, but with a sudden, fierce urgency that surprised them both.

Helena pressed closer, and Paul's hands found her waist, steadying, anchoring.

The kiss deepened – raw and tender all at once – there in the soft, forgiving dark of the car park, with only the old Datsun and the stars to witness.

For a long moment, there was nothing but them and the quiet thrum of everything unspoken between them.

When they finally pulled apart, breathless and smiling, Helena rested her forehead against his.

"Guess you're good with more than just engines," she whispered.

Paul laughed quietly, the sound low and full of something he hadn't felt in a long time: hope.

Neither of them said anything more. They didn't need to.

One night, one kiss, had changed everything.

The call came late, just as Paul was leaving the law library – a blur of folders tucked under one arm, Helena's soft laugh still lingering from their afternoon coffee.

It was David's number, but Allegra's voice crackled through the speaker – sharp, breathless, the background alive with tropical music and the crash of distant surf.

"David's here too," Allegra said quickly. "We need to talk."

Paul frowned, pressing the phone tighter against his ear.

"Talk about what?"

There was a muffled exchange, then David's voice – low, urgent.

"It's Bronwyn," David said. "She's… she's with someone."

Paul blinked, the night thickening around him.

"Some German tourist," David muttered. "Allegra saw them at the resort. They're… not just talking."

Paul leaned back against a cold concrete pillar, feeling the blood drain from his hands.

David's words tumbled faster now, like he was patching holes in a sinking ship.

"Listen, we can fix this. The guy's flying out on Lufthansa tonight. If Allegra keeps Bronwyn busy, we make sure he's gone. No mess. No damage."

A long silence cracked open between them.

Paul stared at the cracked pavement, the forgotten folders slipping from his grasp.

No mess. No damage.

For a moment, he stayed silent, the phone pressed hard against his ear, the sounds of Bali – music, surf, laughter – bleeding into his solitude.

Finally, Paul spoke, his voice low.

"I need to tell you something."

David picked up on the shift instantly, his voice tightening.

"What?"

Paul exhaled slowly, each word feeling heavier than the last.

"I've been seeing someone."

There was a stunned beat of silence.

Then Allegra's voice, sharp and slicing through:

"Who?"

Paul hesitated only a second.

"Helena."

The name hung between them like a lit fuse.

"Helena?" David repeated, disbelieving. "The uni café worker?"

Paul nodded, even though they couldn't see him, shifting his weight against the pillar, the scattered folders like abandoned maps at his feet.

"Yeah," he said simply. "Her."

On the other end, Allegra muttered something – a half-curse, half-sigh – too low for Paul to catch.

David recovered first, but his voice had turned brittle.

"For how long?"

Paul looked out across the empty parking lot, the night endless and cool.

"Since early school start. It wasn't meant to be… it just happened."

Scene: Allegra – The Mocking Headline

Allegra stood alone on the resort balcony, the humid night pressing against her skin. Below, the sounds of laughter, clinking glasses, and slow tropical music floated up, but she barely heard them. Her thoughts were elsewhere – sharp, bitter, slicing through her like broken glass.

She picked up a cocktail napkin from the table, smoothing it against the rail. With a sardonic smile, she pantomimed writing across it, as if scripting tomorrow's social page.

Raising the imaginary newspaper to the empty air, she announced with theatrical cruelty:

"The Farmer No Longer Wants a Wife."

She paused, letting the invisible headline hang, letting it twist the knife.

"From country boy to café girl – Melbourne's golden girl left holding a cocktail umbrella."

Her voice dripped disdain, every word sharpened to a point.

For a fleeting moment, Allegra's face softened – not with sympathy, but with something sadder: calculation, regret, inevitability. Then the hardness returned, snapping back into place like armour.

She crushed the cocktail napkin into a tight ball and threw it over the railing.

"She'll be humiliated, David. Brutally. They'll eat her alive."

Her words were cold, factual – not a warning, but a prediction. A battlefield briefing.

David stood a few steps away, silent, shadows hiding the lines of exhaustion around his mouth. Allegra barely looked at him.

She turned back toward the dark, endless ocean.

"We talk," Allegra said briskly, wiping emotion from her voice like smudges from glass. "We get them back – private restaurant, quiet room. Make them confess. Make them agree to stop. Especially Paul."

Her fingers tapped restlessly on the balcony rail, as if already orchestrating the meeting in her mind.

David cleared his throat, voice rough.

"What if he doesn't?"

Allegra's mouth twitched – not a smile exactly, more a grim tightening.

"He knows the code," she said simply.

Then she turned away, the cocktail lights catching in her hair, and left David staring after her, the faint thud of the crumpled napkin hitting the ground below a quiet, final punctuation.

End of Part One

Part II – The Law of Compassion
Kimberly Doors (née Brady) – The Law of Becoming

At Monash, graduation wasn't a ceremony – it was a machine.

Students moved through Robert Blackwood Hall in careful formation, like parts on a gleaming conveyor belt of ambition. Ushers in crisp suits directed them into lines; robed academics presided from the stage with solemn efficiency. Name after name echoed through the massive space, each called, congratulated, and processed into the world beyond.

Kimberly moved through the line with effortless grace, her honours sash bright against the sea of black. When her name was called, there was a pause – barely perceptible – a nod from the Chancellor. It was recognition. It was respect.

James shuffled along the line behind her. When his name boomed out, it was met with polite, obligatory applause – no pause, no special nod. He smiled tightly for the photo, clutching his degree like a boarding pass to a destination he wasn't sure he still believed in.

Afterwards, in the courtyard, Kimberly found James leaning against one of the tall iron columns, loosening the collar of his shirt.

"You did it," she said brightly, her voice straining against the formality of the day.

"So did you," he answered – but he said it like it hurt.

The Glass Doors of Brady & Sanderson

The glass doors of Brady & Sanderson gleamed under the morning sun, a perfect mirror for the wide, expectant faces that gathered outside.

Twenty new graduates stood at the threshold, blazers sharp, shoes shining, résumés polished to a mirror finish – or at least, that's how they wanted to appear.

Among them were Kimberly and James, fresh from Monash University, carrying the invisible scars and triumphs of their law school years. Kimberly wore her honours degree like hidden armour; James carried the quiet knowledge that he had made it here – even if the path had been bumpier than he'd hoped.

This year, Brady & Sanderson had expanded its graduate intake significantly. They were investing heavily in the future: twenty new graduates across the firm, six in their prestigious Commercial and Litigation division alone.

It was a statement: Growth. Ambition. Renewal.

It was also a gauntlet.

The Partner Speeches: A Glimpse of Glory

The graduates were ushered into the grand Brady & Sanderson boardroom, a space so polished it seemed to hum with power.

Heavy wooden walls, sleek glass partitions, leather chairs – it was a cathedral for commerce and litigation.

Kimberly sat forward in her seat, a fresh notebook open in front of her. James slouched a little, trying to appear relaxed, but his foot tapped under the table.

The Managing Partner Alexander Brady everyone knew James father, a silver-haired man with a voice built for courtrooms, took the podium first.

"You are the future of Brady & Sanderson," he said, his words rich with promise. "This firm has stood for excellence, tenacity, and vision for over forty years.

We expect no less from you."

There was a quiet, electric thrill in the room.

They had made it here – they belonged.

The next speaker was a younger partner from Commercial Litigation, sharp-eyed and fast-talking.

"Your degree got you through the door," she said. "Your grit and adaptability will keep you here. We want thinkers, leaders, team players. Be ready to listen, learn, and most importantly – add value."

Kimberly scribbled notes furiously. James just nodded, already feeling a knot of tension in his gut.

They could feel the gravity of it – opportunity so close they could almost touch it.

Ms Harrington, the Office Administrator

A small woman with steel-grey hair pulled into a tight bun, Ms Harrington wore an expression so stern it could carve marble.

She didn't step up to the podium.

She simply walked to the centre of the room, clipboard in hand, and began without ceremony.

"First, no food at desks. Coffee cups must have lids. Second, no mobile phones visible in client areas. Third, punctuality is not optional. Late three times and you will be reported. Fourth, dress codes will be enforced strictly – navy, black, or charcoal suits only. No exceptions."

Kimberly stopped mid-note-taking, blinking.

James glanced at her sideways, fighting the urge to laugh.

"Fifth, and most importantly," Ms Harrington continued, "you are not special. Every partner, associate, and client expects your utmost professionalism at all times. If you are unsure about something – ask. Mistakes are not appreciated. Discretion is non-negotiable."

The hopeful energy from the partner speeches drained a little.

Reality, sharp and bureaucratic, had arrived.

Ms Harrington handed out printed copies of the Office Code of Conduct, dropping the heavy bundles onto the table with military precision.

No one dared make a sound.

Kimberly tucked the code of conduct carefully into her satchel.

James shoved his into his bag haphazardly, muttering under his breath,

"Welcome to Brady & Sanderson."

Kimberly smiled grimly.

This was just the beginning.

The Associates' Advice

Three associates entered next, their manner casual but their eyes knowing.

Hannah Patel from Commercial Litigation, Marcus Liu from Insurance & Risk, and Jessica Tran from Mergers & Acquisitions.

They perched on the table edges and spoke with the bluntness of soldiers talking to fresh recruits.

"The first six months will be like nothing you've experienced," Jessica said.

"You'll question if you're good enough. That's normal."

"Mistakes will happen," Marcus added.

"Own them. Fix them fast. Hide nothing."

Then came the assignments:

- Kimberly was placed under Jessica Tran, straight into the fire of M&A deals – high-stakes, high-speed.

- James would report to Marcus Liu in Insurance Litigation – methodical, rule-driven work, but a real chance to build his craft.

Their careers were beginning, shaped already by invisible hands.

The First Day: Work Begins

On Monday morning, the glass doors hissed open again as Kimberly and James entered – this time not as guests, but as employees.

Kimberly wore a navy suit so sharp it could slice air. Her ID badge glinted proudly.

James wore charcoal grey, one hand fiddling nervously with his watch strap.

In the open-plan graduate cluster, Kimberly found a neat stack of documents waiting for her:

Due Diligence Review – Client: Solvex Pty Ltd – Report Required COB Thursday.

A sticky note from Jessica read:

"Dive in. See what you can find. Summarise risks."

James's inbox pinged with his first task:

Prepare Draft Letter of Advice – Motor Vehicle Claim Dispute – Supervisor: Marcus Liu.

He opened the attached file: twenty pages of confusing case notes, witness statements, and technical jargon.

For a long moment, neither of them moved.

The hum of keyboards, phones, and muted conversation wrapped around them like ocean waves.

Kimberly tapped her pen once, twice, then smiled grimly.

"Welcome to the jungle," she whispered.

James chuckled under his breath, pulled open a fresh document, and started to type.

Young Love: The Spark of Passion

Amid this turbulence, young love often flourishes.

Freed from school's constraints, relationships become deeper, more complicated, and more intoxicating.

It's a time of late-night talks, first shared apartments, grand plans, and sometimes, painful lessons.

The South Yarra Apartment

Their South Yarra apartment was everything they had dreamed of back at Monash, when long nights of studying blurred into long talks about the future.

High ceilings. Floor-to-ceiling windows. A tiny balcony with a view that caught the last blush of sunset over the Yarra River.

It was too expensive – but just barely within reach if they both budgeted carefully and pretended their battered second-hand furniture was 'vintage'.

James had accepted the graduate role at Brady & Sanderson without so much as a formal interview – a silent handshake behind closed doors, the invisible architecture of family legacy. He hadn't questioned it. Not then. But this place, this life with Kimberly – that had to be different. He didn't want their home to be another gift from Alexander Brady. He wanted it to be theirs.

And Kimberly? She had earned every inch of it. She'd applied for the role like everyone else – résumé, interview, writing task – and not once had she leaned on her relationship with James. If anything, being his girlfriend had made her more cautious, more determined to prove she belonged. His position had been quietly guaranteed. Hers had not. And that made all the difference.

The rent pinched, but the feeling of building something together made it worth it.

The Evenings They Lived For

After the work was done – laptops snapped shut, court judgments bookmarked – the energy shifted.

They would stretch out across the too-small couch, feet tangled, laptops abandoned.

Soft music or the hum of late-night trams filled the background.

There was no need for words.

James would trail his fingers lazily over Kimberly's arm as she scrolled mindlessly through her phone.

Kimberly would curl against him, cheek resting against his chest, the steady thump of his heart grounding her in a way no achievement at work ever could.

Their intimacy wasn't just passion – though there was plenty of that, reckless and unashamed, the way only young love can be.

It was trust, safety, and the certainty that after all the chaos of the outside world, this bond – this small, sacred space between them – remained untouched.

Sometimes, they made love slow and soft, like a conversation without words.

Other times, it was urgent – a way of reminding themselves they were still alive, still young, still each other's in a world that often made them feel small and replaceable.

In those moments – in the crumpled sheets, in the soft gasps against each other's skin – they didn't have to be perfect graduates or rising stars.

They were just Kimberly and James:

- Two dreamers,
- Two fighters,
- Two hearts learning how to survive – and to thrive – together.

Afterwards, tangled in the aftermath, they would whisper about silly things: future holidays they couldn't afford yet, dream houses by the coast, puppies, books they would write someday.

The future felt close when they held each other like that – not easy, but possible.

The Morning Everything Changed

Life at Brady & Sanderson had settled into a rhythm – fast, exhausting, but familiar.

- Kimberly had carved a reputation for herself in M&A, known for sharp instincts and a relentless work ethic.
- James had finally found his stride in Insurance Litigation, earning the respect of his team and a quiet pride that hadn't come easily.

Their South Yarra apartment still felt like home – battered furniture, the stubborn coffee stain on the carpet near the balcony, shared Sunday mornings in bed with legal textbooks pushed to the floor.

They weren't kids anymore.

They were building something real.

But even the best-laid plans have a way of shifting when life decides otherwise.

It started small.

Kimberly, usually regimented and ruthlessly organised, frowned one morning as she scrolled through her phone's calendar, sitting on the edge of the bed in an oversized hoodie.

James was in the kitchen, burning toast again.

"Kimberly? You all right?" he called.

"Yeah," she answered too quickly, forcing a smile that didn't quite meet her own reflection in the window.

The truth gnawed at her quietly:

She was late.

Really late.

But it had been a stressful month – two live deals collapsing, partners breathing fire down her neck, James pulling back-to-back court dates.

It was probably just stress. It had to be.

She told herself that once, twice, a hundred times.

Scene: Tea and Toast

The kettle clicked off with a soft snap. Steam curled up the kitchen window, blurring the view of grey sky over South Yarra. Kimberly poured the hot water over the teabags, letting the scent of English Breakfast fill the silence.

James sat at the counter, tapping his phone with one hand and buttering toast with the other. He hadn't shaved. His tie was still draped over the back of the chair.

"Tea," Kimberly said, sliding his mug across.

"Lifesaver," James muttered, eyes still on the screen.

She sat opposite him, fingers wrapped around her own mug, watching the toast steam between them.

"James," she said quietly.

He looked up.

"I've been thinking about applying to Legal Aid."

A pause. His toast hovered mid-air.

"You serious?"

She nodded. "Just one or two cases. Something outside the glass towers and term sheets."

James set the toast down. "You know that's… not encouraged by the firm."

"But it's not denied either," she said evenly.

He didn't respond. Just stared at the toast like it might offer him a better answer.

"I mean," she went on, "what if we both did something? Something good. Real. For the community. Even part-time."

James leaned back in his chair. The idea hung in the air like steam off their mugs.

“Not me,” he said finally. “That’s not my path.”

She studied him. The set of his jaw. The way his tie remained untouched behind him, like he hadn’t quite put himself together yet.

“Someone still has to pay the bills,” he added, quieter this time.

Kimberly didn’t argue. She just nodded slowly, sipping her tea. The window was fogged over now. Nothing outside but outlines.

But inside, the line between them had been quietly drawn.

The Day of the Test

The sickness woke her before sunrise.

A heavy nausea clamped down out of nowhere, folding her into herself.

She stumbled to the bathroom, hand over her mouth, body shivering.

James jolted awake to the sound of retching.

In two strides, he was kneeling beside her, one hand on her back, the other brushing hair from her face.

“Hey, hey… it’s okay. I’ve got you.”

Kimberly wiped her mouth, breathing hard, resting her forehead against the cool tile.

She didn’t need a doctor to tell her.

Somehow, in the pit of her stomach – deeper than the nausea, deeper than the fear – she knew.

James helped her sit back against the wall, eyes searching hers, wide with concern.

“You’re sick. We should get you checked out. Maybe it’s food poisoning or…”

His voice faltered as he saw the tears brimming in her eyes.

"James…" she whispered, voice breaking. "I'm late."

There was a beat of silence.

Then another.

And then James, wonderful, loyal James, did the only thing he knew to do:

He reached for her hand and held it tightly, anchoring them both to the moment.

"Whatever this is," he said quietly, his thumb brushing over her knuckles, "we'll face it together."

Outside, the city was beginning to stir – trams rumbling awake, the first coffee shops unlocking their doors.

But inside their little South Yarra apartment, everything had already changed.

Kimberly and James: A Promise Made

It was a grey Saturday when they finally faced it properly.

Kimberly sat cross-legged on the bathroom floor, the slim plastic pregnancy test stick lying on the edge of the bathtub.

James paced back and forth just outside the door, too restless to sit, too respectful to crowd her.

The result came quickly – too quickly – but it was unmistakable.

Two lines.

Clear. Certain.

Pregnant.

Kimberly's throat tightened.

She wasn't scared exactly – just overwhelmed, flooded by the sudden vastness of what their lives were about to become.

She opened the door, holding the test like a fragile, glowing secret.

James saw her face, her trembling fingers – and he didn't hesitate.

He pulled her into his arms, wrapping her up completely, as if he could shield her from everything coming.

They stayed like that for a long time – no words, just the thudding truth of their hearts beating against each other.

Later, curled together on the couch, the Melbourne afternoon drizzling against their windows, Kimberly traced small circles on James's knee with her finger.

"You know," she said softly, "if you wanted… if you felt we should…"

"Get married," she finished awkwardly, cheeks heating.

James didn't pull away.

He cupped her face with one hand, tilting her chin so she would meet his gaze.

"Kimberly," he said, voice steady, "I want to marry you."

"Oh, I want to marry you. I love you. But let's wait. Cosette didn't rush to the altar – she waited. For peace. For dignity. I want the same for us. I won't marry to hide the baby. So many women have. I understand why. My Nana had to. But I want to hold our child – openly, proudly – with you beside me. She'd be proud of that. I think she would."

The Birth of Sarah Elizabeth Brady

It happened early one Wednesday morning, under a sky streaked with pale Melbourne dawn light.

After hours of slow, painful labour – Kimberly's hands clutching James's like lifelines – the room finally filled with the sharp, sweet wail of new life.

"It's a girl," the midwife smiled, lifting the tiny, wriggling body into Kimberly's arms.

Tears streamed down James's face before he even realised.

He kissed Kimberly's sweat-drenched forehead, whispering over and over:

"You're incredible. She's perfect. You're both perfect."

They named her **Sarah Elizabeth Brady** –

• **Sarah**, for Kimberly's grandmother (Nana),

• **Elizabeth**, a timeless name filled with grace and strength,

• **Brady**, proudly taking James's family name, a new branch blooming from old roots.

In that tiny, sterile hospital room, everything shifted.

Work emails, court dates, targets – they all faded away.

Only this mattered:

A family. Their family.

The Wedding at Oakleigh

They married six months later, in the crisp sweetness of early spring.

The chapel in Oakleigh was small, old, and filled with light – the kind of place where every wooden beam and stained-glass pane seemed to hum with memory.

Kimberly walked down the aisle with Sarah nestled against her hip for the first part – not a traditional bridal procession, but perfect for them.

She wore a simple, flowing ivory gown, her hair loose around her shoulders.

James waited at the altar, suit sharp but eyes misty, holding their daughter in his arms while the music swelled.

The ceremony was short and heartfelt – no grand speeches, no hollow promises.

Only the truth:

"I choose you. I chose you then, I choose you now, and I will choose you always."

Remembering Nana

At the reception – held in a sunny hall tucked behind the chapel – Nana's picture sat on a small, decorated table by the entrance.

A soft, smiling photo of her at Kimberly's law graduation, corsage pinned proudly to her blouse.

She had passed away just a few months earlier –

A quiet but devastating loss.

There was a simple card next to her photo:

"Forever with us in spirit, forever in our hearts."

Guests paused as they entered – some touching the frame gently, others bowing their heads briefly in respect.

Kimberly's eyes welled up when she passed it the first time, but she smiled through the tears.

Because Nana was there – not in body, but woven into every laugh, every hug, every glance toward the future.

Paul Avery – Every Family Needs a Lawyer

The Weddings – Seen from the Crowd

Paul married Helena two years after law school. There were two ceremonies – one for her family, one for his. The Greek Orthodox service was rich with incense and ancient ritual. The civil ceremony behind the Shepparton library was filled with sunlight, sponge cake, and acoustic guitars.

Behind them, his mother sat between Helena's aunts – who had decided, after one look at her shoes, that she was *proper*.

A week later, the same aunties sat in plastic chairs at the Shepparton hall, clapping along to a cousin's guitar. Paul's father wore a blazer Helena had pressed. The same faces now laughed at *Paul's* jokes. They ate *his* mum's sponge cake.

Two weddings.

Two rituals.

One community, now watching him with new eyes.

After they married, Paul settled into legal work in the Melbourne courts. Not the marble ones upstairs – but the bottom floors. The gritty rooms with coffee-stained tiles, where shoplifters and drink drivers sat beside their overworked legal aid reps.

He was an associate at a big firm, technically. But no billboards bore his name. His job was to hold the lower courts together – the money from those cases kept the wheels turning upstairs, where high-end litigation waltzed through with suits and swagger.

Paul learned early that the best lawyers weren't always the ones in the spotlight. They were the ones who listened. Who knew the rules and when to bend them. Who didn't flinch when a mother cried or a son lied.

He learned this from Michael Forsyth – a partner nobody talked about in glossy brochures, but who could dismantle a case with a raised eyebrow and a single question. Michael had grown up in Coburg, worked two jobs through uni, and still packed a tuna sandwich in a paper bag every day. He never aimed to make partner. He aimed to make sense.

"We're not here to win," Michael once told Paul. "We're here to help people walk away with something they can live with."

So when Theo – Helena's brother – called needing a lawyer, Paul wasn't surprised.

He'd been doing this work for years. Just never for *them*.

Theo's Call

The call came at eight three a.m. Paul had just stepped into the Broadmeadows Magistrates' Court, coffee still too hot in his hand, when his phone buzzed.

"Mate," Theo said breathlessly. "I need you."

The story tumbled out: a Datsun 200B – Helena's old car, now turbocharged by Theo and his mechanic mates for reasons still not fully understood – clocked at 140 km/h on the Western Ring Road. A moment of thrill, a heavy foot, and now a court summons. Reckless driving. Possible impound. License gone. Maybe worse.

Paul exhaled. "All right. I'll be there."

Later that morning, Paul stood beside Theo in front of the magistrate. Calm. Focused.

"Your Honour, yes – the speed was excessive. But this wasn't a joyride. The car is more aspiration than a machine. It barely holds the road. My client misjudged – but he accepts responsibility."

The magistrate softened. A reduced fine. No suspension.

Outside, Theo was shaken but grateful. "Man… I didn't know what else to do."

Paul gave him a look, but didn't say anything.

Theo clapped him on the shoulder, grinning. "You know what? Every family needs a lawyer. Lucky for us, we've got one who married in."

Paul just shook his head, but couldn't help smiling.

Marko's Avery Call.

Markos didn't ask for help the way most people do. He just rang Paul late one evening and said, "The SPC cannery's going under. They're going to shut it. Sell it off."

Paul could hear the wind through the receiver – Shepparton always whispering, even in stillness.

"We want to buy it," Markos said. "A co-op. For the community. For the growers."

Paul waited.

"We're farms, not lawyers. We need your help, mate."

Paul took time off – just a few weeks – to do some private work back home in Shepparton. The kind of legal consulting that didn't involve court filings or barristers in robes, just people who needed things sorted: contract disputes, leases, water rights, quiet divorces.

It was Friday, and they were already packed. Helena had the boys' pyjamas rolled tight into their backpacks. The snacks were sorted, the car fuelled, the windows half-down in the cool dusk air. The two boys – four and five – were bouncing between the front door and the boot, yelling about lollies and who got to sit behind Mum.

They drove out of the city with the sun dropping behind them. The freeway opened wide by Kalkallo, and Paul finally relaxed, one arm draped across the steering wheel.

Helena turned to him and smiled. "You're not going to check your emails this weekend."

"No," he said. "Just contracts and cousins."

The boys fell asleep just outside Nagambie. Helena unwrapped sandwiches she'd made that morning, and Paul ate his with one hand on the wheel, driving into familiar country.

By the time they reached the farm gate, the stars were out and the porch light was on. Markos had left a note stuck to the door: '*Beds made. Milk in fridge. Don't touch the shiraz – it's mine.*'

Paul laughed quietly and tucked the boys into bed.

Later that night, everyone in the family gathered around the big kitchen table. Markos and his wife were already there – she had made a lentil salad and was stacking plates while Helena brought in a tray of cut fruit. Markos poured wine for Paul and grinned.

"They're city kids now," he said, nodding toward the sleeping boys. "You'll have to toughen them up before harvest."

Paul's mother – still living on the farm, his father having passed away from a heart attack two years earlier – was in her element.

She pinched Helena's cheek and insisted she sit.

"You've done enough, *koukla* – that's what your mother would say, isn't it?" she added, nudging Helena into the chair.

The welcome was warm, familiar, easy – a chorus of accents, old jokes, and second helpings.

Markos didn't have children – not yet, maybe never – but he loved having his nephews on the farm. He gave them slow tractor rides in the early morning mist, lifted them up to reach the chook shed latch, and let them collect warm eggs in tiny baskets. He didn't say much about it, but Paul could see it in his face – the longing.

His wife noticed too. She watched them with a soft smile, then turned quickly to hang tea towels in the sun.

Markos let the boys ride the quad bike with him that afternoon and pretended not to notice when they smuggled biscuits into their gumboot pockets.

The weekend stretched ahead: tractors, sun, footy on the radio, Helena cooking lunch with his mum, and maybe a slow walk through the orchard.

On Saturday evening, Helena decided to cook moussaka – her version, which Paul had jokingly nicknamed 'pasta without pasta.' It was for the Baxters, old friends from the next property over who used to play footy with Paul's dad.

The kitchen filled with the smell of cinnamon and roasted eggplant. Helena layered the béchamel with precision while Paul's mum sliced cucumbers from the garden. The boys were barefoot, trailing toy trucks under the table. They weren't in high chairs anymore – old enough now to sit at the table, legs dangling, napkins askew. And they already knew what moussaka was.

"It's yummy, Grandma," the older one said, mouth half-full. "It's like pasta but not pasta."

Paul's mum raised an eyebrow and looked at Helena with mock seriousness. "You've trained them. This is dangerous."

Helena grinned. "They like the cinnamon."

When the Baxters arrived, Helena greeted them with a warm hug and handed off two glasses of wine before they'd even taken their coats off.

Paul's mum leaned in and whispered proudly, "She cooks like my mother did – but better. Don't tell her that."

Then, inspecting the dish more closely, she furrowed her brow and leaned toward Helena with curiosity. "But koukla, how do you make pasta without pasta?"

Helena laughed, wiping her hands on a tea towel. "It's moussaka. The layers are eggplant, potato, and béchamel. The trick is you don't miss the pasta."

The Baxters had never eaten anything like it. Mr Baxter poked gently at the cinnamon-topped slice, then took a bite and immediately looked at his wife.

"We've been doing dinner wrong for twenty years," he declared.

More laughter, more wine. Seconds all around.

Laughter filled the room. The food disappeared quickly. The Baxters left with leftovers, hugs, and a standing invite.

That night, Paul sat on the back steps with Helena, arms around each other, watching the paddocks breathe in the dusk.

"This," he said quietly, "is my favourite kind of court."

Shepparton Public Hall

By Sunday night, Paul was already thinking about Monday.

He had appointments booked with local growers and suppliers – quiet men with sun-worn hands and furrowed brows. They spoke plainly, and their concerns were always laced with a deeper fear: that what their parents built was about to be taken.

On Tuesday morning, he sat down with two old friends from the co-op board. That's when he heard the full scope – SPC was pulling out. Production would be wound down within months. Processing contracts were ending. No transition. No buyback offers.

Paul drove back to the farm, quiet behind the wheel.

That night, under the verandah, Markos poured them both a scotch and said, "We're going to lose everything if we don't act."

Paul nodded. "We'll call a meeting."

By Friday, they'd booked out the Shepparton Public Hall. Word had already spread – by tractor, by bakery, by the back corner of the grocer's counter.

The room filled quickly. Fold-out chairs scraped linoleum. Markos and his wife arrived early and took seats near the front, quietly observing. They were farmers, after all – among the first who would be directly affected. Helena came in shortly after, in a soft country dress, sleeves rolled, calm and radiant. She wasn't there to speak, but her presence anchored Paul.

Paul's mum had stayed behind at the farm to watch the boys. The Averys had dropped by earlier to lend a hand, and by mutual understanding, Mum Avery was now on biscuit patrol. The boys would be fine. Paul stood up front beside a whiteboard and a printout of clauses marked in red.

He looked out at the room – not at strangers, but at faces he knew: the man who helped his father fix an irrigation line, the woman who once gave Helena quinces from her tree, the couple who always waved from their ute.

He cleared his throat.

Before he spoke to the crowd, Paul had done what he always did – the due diligence. As the appointed representative of the local buyer group, he had every legal right to inspect the books. Under the Corporations Act and in accordance with pre-sale disclosure expectations, the current owners granted him access.

But Paul didn't do it alone. He retained a trusted local accounting firm – a Shepparton business that had worked with growers and processors for decades. He sat down with them and reviewed every document in detail, line by line. He wanted transparency. He wanted it verified by people the community already trusted.

He was thorough. Line-by-line. He wasn't there to be impressed – he was there to understand. The viability, the risks, the opportunities. This was business, yes, but it was also law. And he wasn't going to let his town step blindly into anything.

What he found was troubling, but not beyond repair: a loss-heavy last quarter, mismanaged supplier contracts, deferred maintenance schedules, and a back-office system that hadn't been modernised in a decade. Worse still, there were signs of conflicting interests – a proposed sale to an overseas buyer that hadn't been formally announced, but had left fingerprints in the financials and board minutes. If true, it meant the closure wasn't just a cutback. It was a set-up. But the bones were solid. The infrastructure was good. And the brand still had value.

Paul had built his case with facts, not sentiment. That's what would carry the room.

But he also knew the facts weren't enough.

He looked out again at the cannery workers, growers, drivers, admin staff, mechanics – and then he said:

"You've always done the work. You've kept this place running longer than any executive or board member ever could. But if we do this – if we buy it – you're no longer just farmers, cannery staff, or truck drivers."

He paused.

"You become owners. And owners have responsibilities. It means learning new things. Making tough decisions. Planning not just for harvest – but for budgets, payroll, compliance, risk."

The room was still.

"If we do this, you're not employees. You're the board. The backbone. And if we get it right – you're also the future."

A beat. Then he added softly:

"I'll help. I'll guide the structure. But I won't carry it alone. No one can."

That's when the first head nodded. Then another. Then the room followed.

Markos stood up next. He didn't say much. He didn't have to. "We're in," he said, gesturing gently toward his wife beside him. "We've got the cash ready. We believe in this."

A small ripple of movement passed through the crowd.

Then, from halfway back, someone else stood – a woman in a navy blue cannery polo with calloused hands and a tired expression.

"I don't have it all yet," she said, voice steady. "But I can do half now, and the rest on a plan. I've worked here fifteen years. I'm not walking away."

Paul nodded to her with quiet respect. "That's exactly what this is about. We'll work with you. The accounting firm will help sort the structure for each of you. No one's doing this alone."

Paul let the silence settle, then continued.

"Everyone in this room will need to take a financial stake in the business. Not a donation. Not a gesture. A real share – with obligations and with rights. That's how co-ops work. That's how ownership works."

He moved toward the whiteboard and underlined a figure twice.

"We've been running at a loss. We all know it. If we're going to turn that around, every part of the system must work – the picking, the packing, the deliveries. If one orchard doesn't supply on time, the cannery stands still. And when the cannery stops, everything stops."

He paused.

"We'll need an average investment per member – that number depends on how many join. We're working on models with the local accounting firm. They'll help you understand the structure, your options, and whether you want to contribute directly or through loan support."

Paul looked over the crowd. "Yes – loans are on the table. Personal, or through a community lending pool. We're speaking with a credit union about managing that side, and the accounting firm will be available this week to explain everything, face to face."

He paused, then picked up the marker again.

He wrote a number clearly on the board: Ten thousand dollars.

"That's the number. Ten thousand dollars. That's what we need from each member of the co-op. That stake gets you in – gives you a vote, gives you a share, gives you ownership. If we get two hundred and fifty members, we hit the base target to purchase the plant and equipment outright, cover the first two quarters of operations, and start turning this thing around."

He turned back.

"I know it's a lot. That's why the loans and payment plans matter. But if you want in – if you want a real seat at the table – this is what we need from you."

He let the words sit.

"No pressure. No hype. Just the truth. That's what this town deserves."

He turned back to the room.

"This isn't charity. It's work. It's risk. It's a chance – maybe the last one we'll get. But if we take it seriously – together – I believe we can make it work."

"I'm not here as a big-city lawyer," Paul said. "I'm here as one of you. And I've read every word of the contract. They're leaving. But we don't have to."

The End of the Chapter – What Paul Considers

The paperwork was signed. The funds were raised. The co-op was real.

Paul stood outside the cannery one last time before driving back to the farm, watching the sun sink behind the shed roofs. It wasn't just saved – it was theirs now. The town's. The growers'. The staff who signed their names on paper and believed in something bigger than a paycheck.

That night, at the farm, Helena was plating up dinner. The boys were already in pyjamas, trailing jam on the floor. Markos helped clear the table. Paul's mother poured red wine, her hands steady and soft.

Paul hadn't seen his family live like this before. So alive. So free. Helena, glowing in her quiet joy. His boys, dirt-streaked and smiling. Even Markos – calm, grounded, quietly proud.

He considered it. Staying. Leaving Melbourne behind. Building something here.

Markos poured him a glass and leaned back against the doorframe.

"You'll always be a farmer," he said. "You're a lawyer – go back to Melbourne. Serve your new community with pride. But never forget who raised you."

Paul didn't answer. Not yet. But he smiled, and it stayed with him.

Later, as he rinsed dishes with Markos and listened to the boys thumping down the hallway, he let the thought drift across his mind again – not as a plan, but as a maybe. A small practice in Shepparton. One room, maybe two. Real work. Local hands. No trains, just dusty boots on floorboards. The idea didn't frighten him. It felt… possible.

Kimberly and Paul – Eight Years Between Sandwiches

The sandwich shop sagged beside Broadmeadows Magistrates' Court – all cracked vinyl chairs and greasy smells, the sort of place you ended up in when you were too tired to care.

Paul Avery pushed open the door, letting the heavy air wash over him.

He wasn't expecting much – a sandwich, maybe a coffee that hadn't been burnt to death.

He definitely wasn't expecting her.

Kimberly.

Sitting alone at a corner table, a half-eaten chicken salad sandwich on a paper tray, a *Grisham* paperback open in her hands.

Her black jacket was slung over the back of her chair, case files stacked neatly on the seat beside her – forgotten, at least for now.

For a second, Paul just stood there, feeling the years crack open inside him.

He walked over slowly, stopping by her table.

He tapped the corner of her book lightly with his finger.

"Great book," he said, his voice roughened by surprise.

Kimberly looked up – and smiled.

That smile he remembered too well – small, knowing, a little mischievous.

Without missing a beat, she said, "Everyone needs a good lawyer."

Paul chuckled, sliding into the seat across from her like it was the most natural thing in the world.

"Some of us more than others. Especially that kid," he said, nodding toward her files.

She closed the book gently, setting it aside.

For a moment, they just looked at each other – the noise of the sandwich shop, the crackling radio, the clatter of plates – fading into a soft hum.

Eight years gone in a blink.

But here they were again.

Different rings on their fingers.

Different lives packed neatly behind their smiles.

Kimberly set the *Grisham* book down carefully, leaning back with the kind of easy grace Paul hadn't seen in her for a long time.

"This isn't your patch," he said to Kimberly. Not unkind, but clipped. Curious. Guarded.

She took a sip of her coffee, then said evenly, "Just had a mention hearing. Thought I'd grab a bite before heading back to the city."

She stirred her coffee absentmindedly.

"You know, people at the markets are still talking about you. Especially my father."

Paul blinked, caught off guard.

"Me?"

"Yes. The SPC Cannery deal."

She smiled – small, proud. "It was a big thing down there."

He shrugged, a little embarrassed.

"It wasn't much. Just contracts. Paperwork."

Kimberly leaned forward slightly, elbows on the table.

"Not to them," she said. "You saved half the growers from going under. You kept families in business. That kind of thing doesn't make the news in the city, but out at the markets?" She shook her head. "They haven't stopped talking about it."

Paul looked down at his sandwich, pushing it around on his plate.

"It's not like it made the Law Institute Journal," he muttered.

Kimberly laughed – low, genuine.

"Maybe not," she said. "But if you ask around the banana shed or the citrus boys, you'll hear it. Old men who haven't agreed on anything since the '80s are all nodding and saying, 'Look what the Avery boy's done.'"

Paul chuckled, lifting his coffee cup slightly.

Kimberly lifted hers too, clinking it gently against his.

"To the Avery boy," she said.

"And all the quiet victories no one else sees."

Kimberly saw the ring on Paul's finger – and Paul saw hers.

James.

Kimberly smiled – not just with her mouth, but with her whole face.

"We have a daughter," she said. "Sarah. She's four. She's… full of questions. She wants to know how everything works – how birds fly, how water becomes steam, why the moon doesn't fall down."

Paul grinned.

"That sounds exhausting."

"It is." Kimberly laughed. "And incredible. She talks all day, sings at the dinner table, and insists on tucking me in sometimes. She loves mangoes, hates socks, and thinks puddles are personal invitations."

He smiled.

"She sounds wonderful."

"She is," Kimberly said softly. "She's changed everything. Things I thought I'd never slow down for – now I can't imagine rushing through them."

Paul nodded, eyes kind.

"I know that feeling."

Kimberly offered a quiet smile.

"I'd love to meet her someday. I heard you married Helena – how is she, Paul? Do you have children?"

"She is…" Paul said softly. "She's not loud or showy, but she sees everything. And she loves like it's muscle memory – no effort, just instinct."

He added with a hint of pride, "We tell the boys they're just like her – strong, kind, quietly fierce."

Then, after a pause:

"You know," he said, "I never really talked to you about Helena."

Kimberly's eyes flicked toward him – calm, measured.

"No," she said. "You didn't."

He nodded once, slowly.

"I love her," he said simply. "I always have. From the beginning."

There was no defensiveness in his voice. Just certainty.

Kimberly didn't look away. She let the silence settle between them.

"She sounds like someone who holds things steady," she said at last.

"She does," Paul replied. "She sees everything. She makes the hard parts easier. The boys light up when she walks into a room."

He paused, then added, softer still:

"So do I."

Kimberly's expression softened – not with longing, not with regret, but something gentler.

A kind of peace.

"I'm glad," she said. "Truly."

Paul's phone buzzed on the table between them – a sharp trill cutting through the quiet.

He glanced at the screen.

"Courtroom Five in ten minutes."

He stood, slipping his phone into his jacket pocket. Kimberly rose too.

"It was good to see you," he said. And he meant it.

She smiled.

"You too."

They hugged – brief, warm, familiar. No promises. No need for more.

Then Paul turned and walked back out into the grey light, leaving behind the scent of coffee, the quiet hum of the sandwich shop, and the woman who once knew him best.

The Brady Family and Friends – Pizza Night in Brighton

The bell above the bakery door gave a cheerful ding as Kimberly stepped inside, slightly breathless.

The bakery was nearly empty, warm with the scent of fresh bread and cinnamon. Behind the counter, Maria looked up and smiled.

"Miss Brady. You just made it."

Kimberly returned the smile. "Wouldn't miss it. I'm here for the Timsuri cake – preordered."

Maria reached into the display fridge and pulled out a white cake box tied with a navy ribbon. "Still slightly warm. Pistachio cream just set."

"It's beautiful," Kimberly said, and meant it. There was something about a cake made with care – something grounding.

Sarah pressed her face to the glass display, pointing. "Mum, can we get the little lemon ones too? For Hugo and Jasper?"

Kimberly hesitated.

"Please?" Sarah added, eyes wide. "Allegra always brings treats."

Kimberly chuckled and nodded. "Two lemon domes, please. And three soft drinks. Raspberry, lemonade, and… orange?"

Maria rang it all up. "Big night?"

Kimberly exhaled with a half-laugh. "Pizza, kids, family, chaos. The usual."

Maria handed her the cake, the lemon domes, and the clinking bag of bottled drinks.

"The best kind of chaos."

Scene: The Setup

The house was already humming when they pulled into the driveway.

James's car was there. Of course it was. He was already home – showered, shaved, and sorting wine glasses.

Kimberly pushed open the door with her elbow, cake balanced carefully in one hand, Sarah dancing behind her with the drinks bag like it was full of fireworks.

From the kitchen came James's voice, amused and calm. "There she is. Right on cue."

"She handed him the cake. "Handle with reverence."

He kissed her cheek. "Always."

The next hour passed in motion:

- Kimberly swapped her work blouse for a navy jumpsuit and tied her hair with a ribbon Sarah picked.
- Sarah changed into her May dress with the sparkly clip – "To match the cake," she said solemnly.
- James arranged glasses, double-checked the wine, and lit the candles.
- Kimberly folded linen napkins with casual precision, placed the lemon domes on a side plate, then opened the back doors to let the late light in.

Outside, the sky softened into apricot.

The first breeze of evening rolled through the house.

And somewhere between slicing lemons and stacking pizza plates, the night began to open – quietly, gently, like a bloom.

Scene: The Arrival

At exactly seven p.m., the doorbell chimed – three soft notes that felt more like a courtesy than a request.

James opened the door to find David and Allegra standing there, flawless as ever. David wore a dove-grey blazer and crisp dark jeans. Allegra was effortlessly stunning in a draped cream blouse and gold flats, her hair perfectly pinned, a polished gift bag in one hand and a box of cannoli in the other.

And behind them – Jasper and Hugo.

The boys looked like they'd stepped out of a boutique catalogue: matching pale-blue linen pyjamas with subtle piping, monogrammed initials on the chest, and bare feet that had somehow stayed spotless. They blinked at James in polite unison.

"Evening," David said smoothly. "Smells incredible."

"You're just in time," James replied, stepping aside. "Come in."

Sarah squealed and ran forward, arms wide. "Hugo! Jasper! You have the same pyjamas again!"

"They're our pizza night ones," Hugo said matter-of-factly.

"They match the sauce," Jasper added.

Kimberly appeared with a tea towel in hand and smiled. "You boys look very grown-up."

"Mum ironed them for fifteen minutes," Hugo said proudly.

Allegra raised an eyebrow. "Ten. He's exaggerating."

Everyone laughed, and the house, already alive with warmth, felt like it had just taken its first full breath of the night.

Scene: The Pizza Brief

Once coats were hung and drinks poured, James slipped into the study and returned holding a single laminated sheet of paper.

"The Brief," he announced with mock solemnity, placing it by the kitchen phone.

Kimberly looked up from arranging the lemon domes. "Allergies noted, preferences checked, the works."

The sheet read:

- **Pepperoni (mild)** – for Jasper, but only if the slices are round.
- **Hawaiian (half)** – for Hugo, pineapple strictly on one side.
- **Margherita** – Allegra's unwavering classic.
- **Vegetarian with artichoke, no mushrooms** – Bronwyn's uncompromising standard.
- **Two plain cheeses** – for the kids, peacekeeping in edible form.
- **Spicy salami with rocket** – for James, obviously.
- **Capricciosa** – David's no anchovies.
- **Kimberly** – "What if I just have whatever's left?" she'd said, half-laughing. So they left her off the list, knowing full well she'd graze across boxes and end up tidying the kitchen before anyone thought to thank her.

James picked up the phone, grinned at Kimberly, and said, "Operation Pizza Night is officially underway."

Victor stood beside him, clutching a crayon and looking very serious. "Daddy doesn't like those yucky fishies on his pizza."

Kimberly kissed Victor's cheek. "Good man. Defending the family honour, one topping at a time."

Scene: Dinner and DVDs

As the pizzas arrived in stacked, warm boxes and the scent filled the house, the kids didn't need asking twice.

Sarah led Hugo and Jasper into the living room, arms full of cushions and blankets. They quickly turned the space into their own cinema, the DVD already humming the animated menu screen. A stack of old favourites waited beside the TV – *The Incredibles, Finding Nemo, Kung Fu Panda.*

Kimberly poked her head in. “Plates only, no hands, and one soft drink each. Clear?”

“Yes, Judge Mum,” Sarah said, already sliding in a disc.

As the kids nestled in with slices on small plates and laughter spilling around the screen, the adults sat down at the dining table. Candles flickered, wine glasses clinked, and the air filled with easy laughter.

David launched into a story from chambers that had Allegra nearly in tears. Bronwyn’s new boyfriend tried to explain why oat cheese was underrated. James and Kimberly exchanged glances across the table – smiles that said *we did it.*

Then James lifted his glass.

“A toast,” he said. “To David Franks. For making partner, and still finding time to iron pyjamas.”

Laughter rippled around the table. David dipped his head in mock modesty.

“I’m a humble man,” he said, then raised his own glass. “And yes – partner. But I’m not done. We’re opening satellite offices. Strategically placed near suburban magistrates’ courts. Real law, real people, real access.”

Allegra beamed.

David looked around the table, pausing just slightly on James and Kimberly. “And we’re hiring. You two should keep your phones close. I might make you an offer you can’t refuse.”

Kimberly raised an eyebrow. “Are you recruiting or reciting *The Godfather*?”

“Both,” David said. “It’s Brighton. We multitask.”

Scene: The Timsuri and the Last Laughter

Eventually, the table quieted. The candles burned lower. James brought out the Timsuri cake, unboxing it like a ceremony. Pistachio cream, marzipan, sponge layers – all flawless.

"Moment of truth," he said.

Kimberly sliced it cleanly, plated it alongside espresso cups and a few spare lemon domes. The grown-ups leaned back in their chairs, loose with wine and warmth, the conversation drifting to old stories and half-finished ideas.

Laughter still echoed, but it was softer now.

In the living room, the television screen had gone dim. The DVD had long stopped playing. Sarah lay curled on one end of the couch, a blanket over her shoulders. Hugo and Jasper were tangled together on cushions – one clutching a soft toy, the other with a half-eaten crust beside him.

Kimberly peeked in and smiled. "All down."

"Victory," James whispered, sipping his coffee.

Allegra yawned delicately. "The mark of a good night."

"Cake and collapse," David said. "Brighton's unofficial motto."

Kimberly raised her cup. "To the ones we love and the ones who've finally stopped talking."

The table laughed once more.

And the house – still glowing from its evening – settled into quiet, like a held breath gently released.

Scene: The Goodbyes

It was nearly midnight when Allegra gently nudged Jasper's shoulder. "Come on, sweetheart."

He stirred, then blinked as she gathered him up. David scooped up Hugo, who instinctively wrapped his arms around his father's neck without waking fully.

"Thanks for everything," David said at the door, his voice low. "It was perfect."

Kimberly nodded. "We'll do it again soon."

Allegra smiled, brushing Sarah's hair away from her face before whispering, "Let her sleep."

Bronwyn and her boyfriend appeared in the hallway just behind them, slipping on coats and thanking James for the wine and the warmth.

"We'll walk from here," Bronwyn said. "It's a beautiful night."

"You two looked good tonight," Kimberly said with a wink.

Bronwyn laughed. "Only because I didn't try too hard, shame."

They all exchanged soft goodbyes – warm hands, quiet laughter.

And then it was just Kimberly, James, and Sarah – still asleep on the couch, the blanket rising and falling with her steady breath.

James turned off the last lamp. Kimberly placed the final wine glass in the sink.

The door clicked shut.

And the house finally exhaled.

Scene: The Carry and the Couch

James crossed the living room and knelt gently beside the couch.

He eased his arms beneath Sarah, careful not to wake her, and lifted her effortlessly. Her head nestled into his shoulder, her hand still curled around the corner of her blanket.

Kimberly watched from the kitchen, elbows resting on the counter, the ache of the day finally setting in.

James whispered, "I'll tuck her in."

Kimberly nodded, her body too tired to speak. She moved to the couch, sat down slowly, then leaned back and exhaled with her whole body.

The cushions welcomed her like an old friend. One shoe still on. Ribbon slipping loose from her hair.

She didn't intend to fall asleep. Just to rest. Just a minute.

From upstairs came the sound of a creaking floorboard – James returning.

He paused in the hallway, saw her curled on the couch, lips parted, soft breath rising and falling.

He smiled. Then crossed the floor, knelt beside her and brushed her hair back gently.

"Pour us a glass of wine, dear," Kimberly murmured, eyes still closed.

James chuckled. "I thought you were asleep."

"One foot still has a shoe. That means I'm technically awake."

He stood and walked to the kitchen, the clink of the glasses a soft percussion in the calm.

James crossed the living room and knelt gently beside the couch.

Kimberly stirred, barely. Her eyes fluttered open.

"You're still here," she whispered.

"Always," he said, voice warm.

She shifted, curled into his side, her hand resting on his chest. He leaned in, brushing her forehead, then kissed her temple.

The kiss moved – slow, unhurried – to her cheek, and then down, to her neck. That place just below her ear. The one he knew she loved.

Kimberly sighed softly, melting into him. Her smile was sleepy, but it was there.

"I thought I was too tired," she murmured.

James smiled against her skin. "You thought wrong."

The house was quiet, the wine forgotten on the table. And in the hush of that soft-lit lounge, the only thing that moved was the slow rhythm of two people who had loved each other long enough to know how to begin again.

Outside, the stars kept blinking.

Inside, love stayed awake a little longer.

Their kisses deepened – never rushed, always known. James touched her like he'd done a hundred times before, and yet like it still meant everything. His hands found her waist, then her hips, drawing her closer until there was no space between the past they'd shared and the present they were living.

Kimberly responded not with words, but with breath. Her fingertips curled behind his neck, her legs shifting to welcome him in. On the couch where their daughter had just slept, where coffee and crumbs lingered, they made room for something older than sleep.

It was not the urgency of youth, but the conviction of history. Of bodies that had memorised each other. Of desire layered with trust, with rhythm, with promise.

James kissed her collarbone and whispered her name like it was both an apology and a blessing. Kimberly pulled him in, soft and firm, a silent *yes* that only he could read.

The night held them, steady and warm, as they loved each other the way only long-held lovers do – fully, gently, and without needing to say why.

And when it was done, they didn't speak.

They just breathed.

And outside, Brighton slept.

Michelle Jarr – Not Perfect. Just Scared

Morning sunlight filtered through the tall windows of Brady & Sanderson, casting elongated shadows across the polished mahogany conference table. The firm's opulent decor spoke of prestige and tradition, yet beneath the surface, currents of tension swirled.

Alexander Brady, impeccably dressed in a tailored suit, stood at the head of the table, a thin file in hand. His expression was one of practised indifference, the corners of his mouth hinting at a sardonic smile.

"*Ah*, the glamour of Legal Aid," he drawled, placing the file before Kimberly. "Keeps our image charitable."

Kimberly met his gaze, her expression unreadable. She reached for the file with steady hands, the weight of its contents yet to be revealed.

"I'll review it," she said simply.

James Brady, seated beside her, observed the exchange in silence. His jaw tightened, a subtle sign of the frustration simmering beneath his composed exterior.

Alexander turned his attention to James, his tone laced with condescension.

"James, perhaps you can assist your wife in navigating the intricacies of this case. After all, it's not every day we grace the courts with such… noble endeavours."

James's eyes narrowed slightly, but he maintained his composure. He offered a curt nod, choosing to let the comment pass unchallenged – for now.

As Alexander exited the room, the atmosphere shifted. The grandeur of the conference room felt colder, the sunlight less warm. Kimberly opened the file, her eyes scanning the initial details of the case.

James leaned in, his voice low.

"He only cares about the firm's image, not the people we represent."

Kimberly closed the file gently, her gaze meeting his.

"Then let's ensure our actions speak louder than his words. But I'll need formal partner approval before I commit."

MELBOURNE LOCKUP – BEHIND COUNTY COURT BUILDING

The air inside was institutional. Sam followed her down the corridor past security. They waited as the buzz door opened. Inside the interview room, Ms Jarra was already seated.

Kimberly didn't speak right away. She observed. Hands clenched. Shoulders braced. Shirt slightly ripped at the collar, bruises yellowing beneath the surface.

Finally: "Ms Jarra, I'm Kimberly Brady. This is Sam McLellan. We're here on your Legal Aid assignment."

Ms Jarra looked up. "The last one said I should just plead."

Kimberly nodded. "I don't decide anything until I hear your side."

Ms Jarra watched them both. Then: "Is he alive?"

"He's in the hospital," Kimberly said. "Stable."

"So that bastard's okay?" Her voice cracked, not with panic – with rage.

Kimberly nodded. "You are too. That matters."

And then the story came out, piece by piece. Years of shared drug use. They used cold together – ice, mostly. And that day, she had used again – with him. A slip. One she hadn't wanted to admit. He'd brought it in. They'd smoked in silence. She told herself it was just once.

"He said, 'I want hot,'" she said. "I knew what he meant. Heroin. I hadn't touched it in over a year. He said it like it was a reward. Or a punishment."

He left for a while. Came back glowing with it. Quiet. Calm. Dangerous. They argued. He asked for money. Accused her of thinking she was better than him. Then, calmly, cruelly, he grabbed her shirt. Tore it. Groped her like he owned her.

"He threw me to the floor. Tried to have me. Like I was just… his."

And then:

"I got up. I don't remember doing it, but I was on my feet. I grabbed what I could. Kitchen knife. First swing – shoulder. He made this sound. Then the blood came, and I panicked. So I went again. And again. Until he sat down or fell – I don't even know. I couldn't move. I just watched it all happen."

Scene: *Boardroom – The R v Jarra Brief*

The firm's senior boardroom had always felt too large. Kimberly sat three chairs in from the end, flanked by associates with sharpened pens and partners with half-distracted glances. Coffee steamed in paper cups. A muted hum of heaters ticked under the table.

At the head of the table, Alexander Brady presided, as always – cold, polished, distant. A man who measured silence more than words.

"Final docket," he said without looking up. "The *R v Jarra* matter. Legal Aid brief. Kimberly has reviewed the file."

The last word landed like a footnote.

Kimberly sat up straighter. Her voice was calm, but it filled the room.

"Subject to partner approval, I recommend we proceed to trial. The client intends to plead not guilty."

There was a beat. Pens paused mid-air. A few younger associates turned to look at her. One leaned back in his chair with the tautness of someone resisting the urge to comment.

"Eight stab wounds, wasn't it?" Hughes asked, his tone edged with doubt.

From somewhere down the table, someone murmured under their breath, "We were assuming a plea. With hard mitigation."

Kimberly didn't flinch. "The victim – her partner – entered her residence high and attempted to force himself on her. There's a medical history. Police records. This wasn't random. It wasn't rage. It was survival."

Hughes raised an eyebrow. "It's still eight stab wounds."

"She stopped him," Kimberly said evenly. "That's what she'll tell the court."

Silence followed – this time heavier, uncertain. No one met her eyes.

"Well," Alexander said coolly, "nothing quite like the glamour of a Legal Aid trial. Always good for keeping our name in the pro bono newsletters."

A few awkward smiles flickered across the table. Kimberly didn't join them.

"You've reviewed the costs?" Alexander asked, tone sharper now.

"Yes. I'll handle preparation and, if the matter remains in the County Court, I'll run it myself. If it's committed, we'll brief counsel. The support team's already scheduled."

"And the outcome if she loses?"

The question hung a moment before James – silent until now – finally spoke.

"If she loses, she loses defending someone who never got heard. If she wins, this becomes a case we remember. Either way, it's the right play."

That silenced the last of the murmurs.

From across the table, Harold Sanderson – sleeves rolled, glasses low on his nose – looked up from his notes. He simply nodded.

Committal Hearing – Melbourne Magistrates' Court, Early Morning

The courtroom was subdued, the wooden benches worn smooth by years of routine. Fluorescent lights buzzed overhead. Kimberly sat at the defence table, a tidy stack of notes and witness reports in front of her. Sam McLellan, beside her, was quietly flipping through the disclosure.

Ms Jarra sat hunched, flanked by a custody officer, her eyes heavy but alert. A Legal Aid solicitor had been present earlier to handle administrative matters, but now Kimberly had stepped in to conduct the committal herself.

The prosecution announced its readiness.

"The Crown proceeds on a charge of intentionally causing serious injury under section 16 of the Crimes Act," the prosecutor stated. "No application to uplift to attempted murder at this stage."

He paused, then continued: "The accused remains in remand custody. Given the seriousness of the alleged conduct and the Crown's concern for community safety, we make no application for bail and request that remand continue until trial directions are set."

Kimberly noted the phrasing carefully. A charge of attempted murder would place the matter squarely in the Supreme Court. For now, it remained in the County Court's jurisdiction – but that could change, depending on how the Crown interpreted intent and evidence. She knew the DPP sometimes waited until after committal to consider such moves.

She stood and addressed the magistrate: "Your Honour, the defence requests that two of the police witnesses be required for cross-examination under section 37."

The magistrate, a lean man with half-moon glasses, nodded. "Granted. Proceed."

Over the course of the morning, Kimberly dismantled inconsistencies with calm precision. Her tone never wavered. She focused on one thing: the context. The power imbalance. The drug use. The trauma response.

At one point, Sam leaned in.

"Statement from Constable Reardon confirms she was taken to The Alfred. Transferred to Melbourne Custody Centre once stable. Under police watch."

Kimberly nodded. "Lines up. She didn't know he'd survived until we told her."

When the magistrate rose at noon for a short adjournment, Kimberly stepped outside to call the firm.

She got Harold.

"Harold, it's likely to stay in County. The brief's solid. She held up well. Committal's continuing, but I think we're going to trial."

Harold paused. "Alexander won't like the billable hour forecast."

"I'm not billing. I'm representing."

Another pause. "Then carry it, Kimberly. We'll back you."

She hung up, then took a deep breath before returning to court.

Dame Phyllis Frost Centre – Legal Interview Room, Late Afternoon

The door clicked behind Kimberly as the officer left them alone. The room smelled faintly of disinfectant and metal. Ms Jarra sat across the small laminate table in pale blue prison-issue sweats, her hands folded tightly in front of her. The bruises had faded, but a haunted weariness clung to her posture.

Kimberly set a folder on the table but didn't open it. "Trial directions are next. You'll stay on remand until then. We're in County Court now."

Ms Jarra didn't look surprised. Just tired. "Will they ever let me out?"

"That depends on the judge. And your history. But for now, they're keeping you in custody. Serious charge, community safety concerns."

Silence settled. Kimberly waited.

Finally, Ms Jarra spoke, voice low: "I haven't used it since they brought me here. First time in years. My head's clearer. That's worse, you know?"

Kimberly nodded. "I believe you."

Ms Jarra blinked, surprised.

Kimberly continued. "We'll need to prepare for trial. I'll be asking for your medical records. And I'll want someone who can speak to your history – someone who knows who you were before the drugs. A neighbour. A teacher. Anyone."

Ms Jarra gave a weak smile. "You think there's someone who remembers me before all this?"

"I think someone does. We just have to find them."

Ms Jarra looked down at her hands. "If I lose, what happens?"

"You'll be sentenced." Kimberly kept her tone steady. "But I don't plan to let that happen without every truth being told first."

A long pause. Then Ms Jarra nodded.

The guard returned to the door. Kimberly rose.

"Next time, we'll talk about your testimony. And about him. All of it."

Ms Jarra didn't speak as she was led away. But she glanced back once, just before the door closed.

That was enough.

County Court of Victoria – Trial Directions Hearing

The courtroom was quiet but expectant, its high ceilings and polished benches lending a cold grandeur to the process. Kimberly sat at the bar table, papers neatly aligned, her robe pressed and collar crisp. She scanned the courtroom as the judge entered, noting the prosecutor – a man in his late forties, experienced and measured – already reviewing his notes.

The judge took the bench and glanced at the file. "R v Jarra. Legal Aid matter. Ms Brady, I understand you're appearing?"

Kimberly rose. "Yes, Your Honour. I appear on behalf of the accused, who remains in custody."

The prosecutor stood. "Your Honour, the Crown confirms the indictment has been filed. We proceed on a single charge of intentionally causing serious injury under section 16. No motion to uplift. All witness statements have been served."

The judge looked to Kimberly. "Has the defence had adequate time to review the brief?"

"We have, Your Honour," Kimberly replied. "We confirm a plea of not guilty. The matter is to proceed to trial."

The judge made a note. "Estimated trial length?"

"Three to four days," the prosecutor offered. Kimberly nodded in agreement.

The judge turned to the associate. "Set down for trial. Matter to return for mention six weeks from today. Custody to continue."

Kimberly gathered her papers as the date was called. The prosecutor leaned over, voice low.

"You sure you want to run this one, Brady? Jury sees eight wounds and shuts off."

Kimberly met his gaze evenly. "Juries listen better than some lawyers give them credit for."

She turned, walked out past the polished pews and legal gowns, already running through the next steps in her mind: medical records, character witnesses, cross-examination prep.

Outside, the cold wind hit her face. She welcomed it. The trial was coming.

East Wing Interview Room – County Court Preparations

The walls of the interview room were bare, the table scarred with initials and scratches from years of waiting. Kimberly sat across from Ms Jarra again – this time post-mention, with trial preparations underway.

A correctional officer waited just outside. The door remained closed, but the atmosphere was more alert now – fewer unknowns, more strategy.

Kimberly placed a plain manila folder between them. "These are your medical records. I've requested everything back to your first rehab. I'll also be calling for your GP and any clinic staff who treated you in the last two years."

Ms Jarra nodded slowly. "The methadone doctor saw me when I was clean. She might remember."

"We'll track her down."

Kimberly opened another document. "And this is your character witness list. It doesn't have to be long – just someone who can say you're more than the person in the brief. Anyone come to mind?"

Ms Jarra hesitated. "Maybe my old neighbour. Mrs Salas. She used to talk to me before it got bad. She saw me trying."

Kimberly wrote it down. "Do you know if she still lives there?"

"I think so. She used to watch my dog when I was at TAFE."

Kimberly looked up. "You studied?"

"Hairdressing. I never finished. But I was good at it."

Kimberly smiled slightly. "That's exactly the kind of detail that matters. It makes you real."

Ms Jarra gave a faint shrug. "They'll still see junkie with a knife."

"Not if we do our job properly. You'll be a person. Not a headline."

Outside, footsteps echoed in the corridor. The officer knocked.

"One more thing," Kimberly said quickly. "We need to talk about how you'll testify. You don't have to, but it might help the jury see the real story. Think about what you're willing to say – and what still feels too raw."

Ms Jarra nodded. "I'll try. I just… I need them to know I wasn't angry. I was scared."

Kimberly gathered the files. "That's what we'll show them."

The door opened, and the officer gestured. Ms Jarra stood, her hands loosely cuffed.

As she was led away, she didn't look back this time – but her pace was steadier.

Kimberly stayed behind, adding Mrs Salas's name to the witness brief, underlining it once in ink.

Dame Phyllis Frost Centre – Interview Room: After the Incident

Kimberly sat at the narrow table across from Ms Jarra. The lighting buzzed faintly above them, and outside, boots echoed along the corridor. The folder in Kimberly's hands was thinner than usual, but it weighed more.

She opened it slowly. "They've filed an incident report. Two weeks ago. You broke another inmate's finger."

Ms Jarra looked away. "She stole my durries. I asked for them back."

Kimberly stayed still. "And then?"

"She laughed. Told me to come take them. I told her she had no right – then she hit me. Right in the face."

Kimberly's voice was flat. "And then you grabbed her wrist and twisted. Broke her finger."

Ms Jarra's eyes flicked up. "She was yelling. She kept swinging at me. I just grabbed her. I didn't mean to break anything."

"You said that before," Kimberly replied quietly. "But the officer's notes say she was trying to walk away when it happened."

A long pause. Ms Jarra's mouth moved like she wanted to explain, but the words didn't come.

Kimberly leaned forward slightly. "Did she break it, hitting you? Or did you do it?"

Ms Jarra's eyes flashed, not with rage – but with something smaller, more jagged. "I broke it. After she hit me. I saw red. I wanted her to hurt."

Kimberly didn't flinch. She closed the folder.

"You lied to me, Jarra."

"I didn't lie. I didn't tell it all."

"Which, in court, is the same thing." Kimberly sat back. "We go forward from here with everything on the table. You understand? No more redacted truth. If I'm going to stand beside you, I have to know what I'm standing on."

Jarra nodded slowly. "I got it."

Kimberly rose and knocked on the door for the guard. As she waited, she turned back.

"That moment at home? That's what this case is about. Not cigarettes. Not prison. Not rage. You forget that again, and no one – not even me – will be able to help you."

The guard opened the door. Ms Jarra stood, cuffed. She didn't look back. But this time, she said clearly, "I won't forget."

Brady & Sanderson – Partner Debrief: The Cost of a Lie

The room was smaller than the senior boardroom but more severe – just a narrow table, four chairs, and a glass carafe of water no one touched. Harold Sanderson was already seated, flipping slowly through a copy of the prison incident report. "Corrections sent it yesterday," he said without looking up. "Clerk flagged it. Thought we should see it before you did." Alexander Brady stood by the window again, unreadable.

Kimberly entered without waiting to be called.

Alexander didn't waste time. "You confirmed it?"

"Yes." Kimberly placed her notes flat on the table. "She admitted it. Not at first, but I pressed. She said it was rage, not fear. Her words."

Alexander nodded once. "So the client lied to her counsel. That's the line."

Harold spoke, voice low but pointed. "No. That's the line if we decide it is. She's still entitled to a defence."

"She's still our client," Kimberly added. "And the original charge remains: intentionally causing serious injury. That incident happened in her home. This" – she tapped the folder – "happened in a cage."

James entered mid-way through, closing the door behind him.

Harold looked to Kimberly. "Can you still run it?"

Kimberly met his eyes. "Yes. I don't trust everything she says. But I believe the truth of the home incident. And I know the difference between damage and intent. I can run it. But I won't pretend the remand incident didn't change the shape of the risk."

Alexander exhaled through his nose. "You'll need to isolate the narratives. Compartmentalise the violence. Show the jury there's a line between trauma and temperament. You think you can do that?"

"I do," Kimberly said.

Harold nodded once, then to Alexander. "We continue. But we're realistic. She lies again, we pull support."

Alexander added, "And no character witnesses unless you're ready for this to come out in open court."

Kimberly gathered the report. "Understood."

Harold said nothing more. He closed his notebook and stood.

The meeting ended without a vote. It didn't need one.

Kimberly left first. She had a trial to prepare.

Opening Statements – Day 1 The Trial

Kimberly Brady stood, robes crisp, hands steady. The courtroom was quiet. Twelve jurors watched her, their expressions a careful mix of neutrality and curiosity. She stepped forward – not behind the lectern, but just to the side of it. Direct, open.

"Ladies and gentlemen of the jury," she began, "you'll hear a lot over the coming days. You'll hear about addiction. You'll hear about a knife. You'll hear about a man bleeding in a kitchen. But before any of that, I ask you to remember something simple: not every truth is clean. And not every person who tells it is perfect."

She let that sit.

Every lawyer in the room knew what had changed. The good character defence – once quietly forming the backbone of her approach – was gone. It had died the moment the remand report landed on her desk. What was left wasn't sympathy. It was survival, stripped to its bones.

"My client, Ms Jarra, is not here today because she is a saint. She is here because on one night, in her home, she was terrified. The man you'll hear about was her partner. They had a long and difficult history – marked by shared drug use, dependence, and control. That night, he entered her space while high. He demanded money. He put his hands on her. He threw her to the floor."

Kimberly's tone remained even.

"She acted. She reached for a knife. She struck. She doesn't remember all of it. She panicked. She stopped when he stopped."

A pause.

"You'll hear the Crown describe her actions as excessive. Intentional. But I'll ask you to consider whether, in that moment, fear overruled everything else. Whether survival – not rage – was what governed her actions. You'll hear about her past. But your task is not to judge who she is. It's to ask whether what she did, in that one moment, was criminal – or human."

She stepped back.

"At the end of this trial, I will ask you to find her not guilty. Not because she's perfect. But because the law allows for imperfection when the truth is complicated, and the fear is real."

She returned to her seat.

County Court – Crown Opening Address

The Crown Prosecutor rose with calm precision. His gown swayed slightly as he moved to the lectern, voice already measured.

"Members of the jury, what you will hear in this courtroom is not a case about self-defence. It is a case about control – about what happens when someone loses it."

He paused, letting his eyes move across the jury.

"On the night in question, the accused, Ms Jarra, stabbed her partner not once, but eight times. In the chest, the shoulder, the stomach. Not in defence of her life. Not to escape. But in anger. In drug-fuelled, chaotic rage."

He lifted a hand slightly. "You will hear about their shared drug use. About an unstable relationship. But those facts do not excuse what happened. The law does not ask you to judge addiction. It asks you to judge actions."

He moved a step closer.

"Ms Jarra had a choice. The victim – though high – was unarmed. He posed no imminent threat of death. He had left the house once that night and returned. There were exits. She could have run. She did not."

The prosecutor opened a file, holding it lightly.

"You will hear from police officers, medical experts and forensic pathologists. Their testimony will be clear: the wounds were deep. They were deliberate. And they did not stop until the victim could no longer stand."

Another pause.

"You may hear that Ms Jarra was afraid. That she acted out of trauma. But I urge you to listen closely – to the number of wounds, the medical evidence, and her own statements. The Crown contends that what she did was not necessary. It was not reasonable. And it was not lawful."

He stepped back.

"At the end of this trial, we will ask you to return the only verdict consistent with the evidence: guilty."

Prosecution Case Begins: Calling the First Witness

Scene: *County Court of Victoria – Day 2 of Trial*

The courtroom was hushed. The prosecutor stood, smoothed the front of his robe, and addressed the judge.

Prosecutor:

"Your Honour, the Crown calls Constable Reardon."

A uniformed officer stepped into the witness box, adjusting his belt as he swore the oath. His tone was professional, clipped – a man used to routine.

Prosecutor:

"Constable, you attended the residence of the accused on the night of the incident. What did you observe?"

Reardon:

"Upon arrival, the accused was seated on the kitchen floor, hands covered in blood. A male was lying nearby, semi-conscious, with stab wounds to the chest and shoulder."

Prosecutor:

"Did she speak?"

Reardon:

"She said, 'I think I killed him.' Then repeated, 'He tried to hurt me.'"

Prosecutor:

"What did you do next?"

Reardon:

"Secured the knife, administered first aid. The ambulance was en route. She was compliant – shaky, but not resisting."

Cross-Examination: Kimberly Brady

Kimberly rose slowly. Calm. Unshaken.

Kimberly:

"Constable, you said the accused was on the floor, blood on her hands?"

Reardon:

"Yes."

Kimberly:

"Did she appear lucid? Intoxicated?"

Reardon:

"Some signs of recent use. But aware."

Kimberly:

"Did she resist arrest? Threaten officers?"

Reardon:

"No. She seemed… devastated."

Kimberly:

"And she said he 'tried to hurt her' – not, 'I wanted to hurt him,' correct?"

Reardon (hesitates):

"That's correct."

Kimberly:

"You entered a home where the only person armed was the accused. Yet you found her seated, bloodied, not fleeing. Did that strike you as odd?"

Reardon (quietly):

"Yes."

She paused, let that sit with the jury. Then moved on.

Kimberly:

"Did you note signs of a struggle? Disarray?"

Reardon:

"Yes. Overturned chair, broken mug, torn shirt near the victim."

Kimberly:

"And no sign of forced entry. He was known to the residents?"

Reardon:

"Correct. He had a key."

Second Witness: Forensic Medical Officer

A calm, experienced woman takes the stand.

Prosecutor:

"Doctor Chen, can you outline the nature of the injuries?"

Dr Chen:

"Eight stab wounds. Varying depths. One grazed the lung, another struck the abdominal muscle wall. The rest were non-lethal but severe."

Prosecutor:

"Would you describe the wounds as frenzied?"

Dr Chen:

"Suggestive of panic. Not all strikes were forceful. Some shallow, some hesitant."

Cross-Examination: Kimberly Brady

Kimberly:

"Doctor, are you saying the wounds were inconsistent with a deliberate killing?"

Dr Chen:

"They lack uniformity. Some were… tentative."

Kimberly:

"And could such wounds be consistent with someone acting out of fear rather than intention?"

Dr Chen:

"That is medically plausible."

Kimberly:

"You noted bruising on the accused's forearms?"

Dr Chen:

"Yes. Defensive wounds."

Kimberly:

"And did the victim have substances in his system?"

Dr Chen:

"Yes. Ice and heroin, both active."

Kimberly stepped back, hands clasped.

Kimberly (to jury):

"Nothing further."

Crown Witness: The Victim Takes the Stand

Scene: County Court of Victoria – Day 3 of Trial

The courtroom shifted the moment he entered.

He wore grey slacks and a pressed white shirt, collar unbuttoned, no tie. Clean-shaven. Hair neatly combed. A faint bandage still visible under his left sleeve. His gait was careful – controlled – but he didn't appear fragile.

As he took the oath, his eyes avoided Ms Jarra's completely.

Prosecutor (rising):

"Please state your name for the record."

Witness:

"Daniel Reed."

Prosecutor:

"Mr Reed, do you recall the night of May 14th of this year?"

Reed:

"Yes."

Prosecutor:

"Can you describe the events leading up to your injuries?"

Reed:

"I visited Michelle's apartment that night. We'd been trying to stay clean. We'd both been doing methadone. But earlier that day… I used. Ice. Then heroin."

He paused, eyes fixed somewhere past the bar table.

Reed:

"I told her. She got angry. Said I was weak. I left. Walked around. When I came back, I asked if she had money. She snapped.

Said I was trying to drag her down. Then she went to the kitchen. I thought she was getting water. But she came back with a knife."

Prosecutor (gently):

"Did you provoke her in any way? Threaten her?"

Reed:

"No. I never laid a hand on her. Not that night."

Prosecutor:

"What happened next?"

Reed:

"She came at me. Said she was sick of being used. And then… she stabbed me. On the shoulder first. I tried to get away. But she kept coming."

He exhaled slowly.

Reed:

"I don't remember how many times. Just the blood. I remember falling. And her crying. But she didn't call for help. I was bleeding out. I thought I was going to die."

The Courtroom Reacts

A murmur swept through the gallery. One juror leaned slightly forward. Kimberly watched carefully, her expression unreadable. She made a few quick notes, then closed the folder gently in front of her.

Cross-Examination: Kimberly Brady

She stood.

Kimberly:

"Mr Reed, thank you. I know recounting these events isn't easy."

A pause. She stepped away from the lectern, voice even.

Kimberly:

"You say you returned to Ms Jarra's apartment after using. Did you tell her what you had taken?"

Reed:

"I said I'd used. She assumed."

Kimberly:

"Is it true that in the past, you've used heroin together?"

Reed:

"Yes."

Kimberly:

"And that when high, your behaviour has sometimes turned… aggressive?"

Reed (tense):

"I never hit her."

Kimberly:

"But you've shouted. Called her names?"

Reed:

"Yeah. We both did."

Kimberly:

"You said she 'snapped' – did she ever say she was scared?"

Reed:

"No."

Kimberly:

"Did you grab her shirt that night?"

A pause.

Reed:

"No."

Kimberly leaned slightly forward.

Kimberly:

"You're sure?"

Reed:

"I told you – no."

She held up a photograph: a ripped shirt recovered from the floor, its collar torn clean through.

Kimberly:

"This shirt was found at the scene. The one Ms Jarra was wearing. Are you saying she did that herself?"

Reed:

"I don't know."

Kimberly (gently but firmly):

"You said you fell and bled. But Constable Reardon testified that you were *seated upright*, conscious, when he arrived. You remember that?"

Reed:

"I… remember being on the floor."

Kimberly:

"Not trying to help her. Not dialling for help. Just sitting."

Reed didn't answer. A flicker of uncertainty crossed his face.

Kimberly:

"Mr Reed, isn't it true that when you asked for money, she refused – and you became angry?"

Reed:

"I was frustrated. Not angry."

Kimberly:

"And that you reached for her? That you grabbed her and said, quote, 'You think you're better than me now?'"

Reed (angrily):

"That's not how I said it."

Kimberly:

"But you did say it?"

Silence.

Reed:

"Yes."

She turned to the jury, letting that resonate.

Kimberly:

"No further questions."

Tension in the Air

Kimberly returned to her seat slowly, her face calm but her jaw set. The judge called for a short recess. As the jurors filed out, Daniel Reed remained in the witness box, rubbing his forearm.

Ms Jarra didn't look at him once.

County Court – Consultation Room, Just Before Testimony

The small side room off the courtroom was plain – white walls, fluorescent light humming overhead, a laminated table between them. On the far wall, a clock ticked with merciless consistency. They had ten minutes. Maybe less.

Kimberly Brady sat forward in her robes, hands folded, eyes locked onto her client's.

Kimberly (measured, direct):

"This is it, Michelle. When you walk in there, everything changes. And I need you to hear me."

Ms Jarra looked pale but composed. She nodded once, eyes flicking to the closed door as if expecting it to fly open.

Kimberly leaned closer.

Kimberly:

"You are not going to talk about your character. Not the good. Not the bad. Not the in-between. Understand?"

Ms Jarra:

"But if they know I tried—"

Kimberly (sharper now):

"No. Listen to me. If you open that door, the Crown will walk straight through it. They will drag out every scar you've ever hidden. Every arrest. Every failed rehab. That fight in remand? It will be the headline. And we won't close that door again."

A pause. Then, gentler:

Kimberly:

"This isn't about proving you're a good person. It's about proving you were scared. That night. In that moment."

Ms Jarra looked down at her hands, her voice barely audible.

Ms Jarra:

"I was scared. But I was also tired. Of everything."

Kimberly (softly):

"Then tell them that. But not like a speech. You talk them through it – like it's happening all over again. Step by step. What you saw. What you felt. What you thought was coming next."

She let that sit. The clock ticked louder in the silence.

Kimberly (calm, resolute):

"You don't need to perform. You don't need to persuade. You need to remember. And tell the truth."

Ms Jarra:

"Even if it's messy?"

Kimberly:

"Especially because it's messy."

A beat passed. Then Ms Jarra nodded. Once. Firmly.

Kimberly reached for her legal pad, tore off a corner of paper, and scribbled a single sentence in her precise hand. She passed it across the table.

Ms Jarra read it:

"Not perfect. Just scared."

She folded it once, placed it in her pocket.

Back to the Courtroom

The guard knocked once. Kimberly stood.

Kimberly (quietly):

"Let's go show them who you were that night. Not the version they think. The real one."

Ms Jarra nodded again, straighter this time. They walked toward the courtroom doors – not as lawyer and client, but as two women stepping into fire with truth as their only shield.

County Court of Victoria – Afternoon Session, Day 3

The air in the courtroom had thickened. No one shifted in their seat. The judge leaned back, hands steepled beneath his chin. Kimberly Brady sat at the bar table, silent, her eyes on the woman in the witness box.

Michelle Jarra sat straight, but only just. One hand clutched the edge of the box; the other rested in her lap, fingers twitching lightly, a nervous rhythm she hadn't even noticed.

The clerk had sworn her in. Kimberly had asked her to speak in her own words.

Now, there was just her voice.

The Testimony of Michelle Jarra

Ms Jarra:

"I wish I could tell you I was clean that day. I wish I could say I was strong. But that wouldn't be the truth."

She looked up – not just at the judge, but past him, toward the jury.

Ms Jarra:

"I'd been clean for four months. Methadone program. Keeping it together. Then Daniel showed up. He had ice – meth. And I said no at first. But I was tired. Tired of everything."

She exhaled, hard.

Ms Jarra:

"I used. With him. That's on me. No one forced me. I chose it. And I hated myself while I did it."

A pause.

Ms Jarra:

"Yeah, it was quiet after we used. Not the good kind. More like before a fight – that still, shaky kind of quiet."

The jury listened without blinking.

Ms Jarra:

"He asked for money. I said no. He laughed. Called me stuck-up, fake, said I thought I was better than him. I told him to leave. He didn't."

Her voice dropped to a whisper.

Ms Jarra:

"He stood over me. I stepped back, but there was nowhere to go. He grabbed my shirt. Tore it. Groped me. Told me I still owed him."

Her hands trembled now. She didn't hide it.

Ms Jarra:

"I pushed him. He shoved back. I hit the floor. The tiles were freezing. I couldn't breathe."

She glanced toward Kimberly – not for permission, but for courage.

Ms Jarra:

"I got up. I grabbed the knife from the sink. I didn't think – I *reacted*. First swing hit his shoulder. He lunged. Or I did. I don't remember. But I kept swinging. Because I thought if I didn't, he wouldn't stop."

Her eyes were wet, but her voice held.

Ms Jarra:

"I didn't want to kill him. I didn't even want to hurt him. I just wanted to not be afraid anymore. I was so tired of being afraid."

A Stillness in the Room

She let that silence hang. Let it breathe.

"When it stopped… I froze. He collapsed. I dropped the knife. I sat at the table. Just… sat. Blood on my hands. All over the floor. I didn't call for help. I couldn't move."

A pause. Her words hang in the silence.

"That's how they found me. Still sitting. Still scared."

She looked up slowly, her voice quieter now.

"I'm not here to explain everything. I can't. But I can tell you what I felt in that moment: fear. Overwhelming, shaking fear."

"That's the truth. Not strength. Not clarity. Just fear. I didn't know what to do. I just needed it to stop."

Scene Close: The Court Reacts

The judge said nothing. The Crown did not immediately rise. The jury sat frozen in their seats – not in sympathy, not in judgment – but in that rare stillness that only truth can command.

Kimberly slowly stood.

Kimberly:

"Your Honour, the defence has no further questions."

The judge nodded once.

Judge:

"Ms Jarra, you may step down. You'll remain in custody pending final arguments."

As the guard approached, Michelle turned once more – not to look at the prosecutor, not even at Kimberly.

She looked at the jury.

And she didn't say a word

County Court of Victoria – Jury Deliberation Room, Day 4

The door shut with a solid thud. The bailiff turned the key and walked away.

Inside, the jury of twelve sat around a long laminated table beneath fluorescent lights. A tea tray sat untouched in the corner.

No phones. No notes beyond what had been handed in. Just paper. Pens. And the charge sheet.

A moment of silence stretched between them – the kind that feels like a held breath.

Then someone spoke.

Juror 4 (mid-50s, public servant):

"Eight stab wounds. That's not nothing."

Juror 8 (nurse, late 30s):

"And a torn shirt. And bruising. And her testimony. That's not nothing either."

Juror 2 (young, uneasy):

"But she used meth. With him. On the same day."

Juror 12 (retired, sharp):

"Didn't deny it. She told us herself. That's something."

They went quiet again. Someone shuffled their notes.

Juror 6 (teacher, analytical):

"I keep coming back to the photograph. The blood pattern. It was everywhere, yes. But she never left. Didn't run. Didn't try to hide the knife."

Juror 1 (foreperson, calm):

"And the kitchen floor. That detail. The cold tile. That wasn't rehearsed."

Juror 9 (sceptical):

"Still. Eight wounds."

Juror 7 (social worker):

"You say it like a number matters more than fear. What if she didn't stop because she didn't know when he would?"

Juror 5 (older man, rarely spoke):

"I think she thought she was going to die."

They Re-read the Charge Sheet

They gathered around the table again, leaning in.

Juror 1:

"The charge is *intentionally causing serious injury*. It has to be intention. Not recklessness. Not panic. Not accident."

Juror 4:

"But if she panicked, it's not intention."

Juror 6:

"Self-defence. She has to believe it was necessary, and the belief has to be reasonable."

Juror 2:

"Then can't we find her guilty but recommend a lighter sentence?"

Juror 1 (sighing):

"I don't think that's an option."

He pressed the intercom. After a few minutes, the judge returned, robed but seated.

In-Courtroom Direction from the Judge

The jury stood.

Foreperson (Juror 1):

"Your Honour, are we allowed to find the accused guilty but recommend leniency?"

Judge (firm, patient):

"Thank you for your question, Mr Foreperson. I understand that this has been a difficult and emotional trial. However, the law requires that your verdict be based solely on the evidence presented, and confined to the charge before you – that is, guilty or not guilty of intentionally causing serious injury.

"You are not permitted to recommend leniency or attach any commentary to your verdict. That is not within your role. If the verdict is guilty, then the matter of sentencing will rest entirely with me, and I will consider all relevant factors at that stage – including any that may be in favour of the accused.

A pause.

Judge:

"You must now return to your deliberations. If you require clarification on any point of law or procedure, you may send a written note via the court officer. I will respond as necessary in open court."

Back in the Jury Room

The door closed again.

Silence. Then:

Juror 8:

"Okay. So it's all or nothing."

Juror 7:

"She told us everything. Even the part that hurt her case. That's not a lie. That's a person trying to be heard."

Juror 4:

"And what if she hadn't fought back? What then?"

Juror 6:

"Then we'd be reading about a dead woman in the Herald Sun. That's what."

A long silence.

Then:

Juror 1:

"Let's vote."

One by one, hands were raised. Hesitant at first. Then more certain.

Final Scene: Courtroom – Verdict

Michelle Jarra stood in the dock, chin low, wrists clasped in front of her. Kimberly stood beside her, impassive but unblinking.

The jury filed back in. The foreperson handed the paper to the tipstaff, who passed it to the judge.

Judge (reading):

"In the matter of *The Queen v Michelle Jarra*, how do you find the accused?"

Foreperson:

"Not guilty."

A quiet gasp from the gallery.

Michelle didn't move. For a second, she didn't understand. Then her knees buckled slightly, and Kimberly steadied her arm.

Judge:

"You are discharged of this indictment. Ms Jarra, you are free to go."

Outside the Courtroom

Michelle stepped onto the steps of the County Court. No cameras. No speeches. Just cold wind and clouds drifting low over Melbourne.

She pulled the old slip of paper from her pocket. *Not perfect. Just scared.* Folded it. Put it away.

And kept walking.

James Brady – The Tomb of Ambition

The office was a tomb of soft lights and hard ambition.

James Brady sat alone at the long mahogany conference table, sleeves rolled up, tie discarded on the floor. Beyond the glass windows, the city pulsed in restless neon.

Brady & Sanderson – the firm built by titans, his father's empire, and James's inheritance…

If he could survive long enough to claim it. He checked the time: six twelve p.m.

His phone buzzed against the wood – a message flashing on the cracked screen.

"Sarah's school concert starts at seven. Joshua's been asking for you all day. Please, James. Just this once."

– Kimberly

James closed his eyes.

Sarah, nine years old, was waiting with her violin.

Joshua, barely two, clutching a plastic truck, searching the doorway.

He thumbed out a reply without thinking.

"I'm sorry. Big meeting. Tell them I love them."

He lied to himself that love could travel through screens – that someday, success would buy back the moments he was trading away.

He turned the phone face down, silencing the next inevitable message.

Chasing the Crown

James wasn't just chasing partnership.

He was chasing independence.

Respect.

Power.

Everyone at Brady & Sanderson remembered whose son he was – the whispers, the sideways glances, the assumption that his seat was reserved, not earned.

Not this time.

The Silvermere case wasn't about duty.

It wasn't about legacy.

It was about conquest.

Every night spent poring through forums, every whispered interview with angry investors, every delicate conversation with insurance insiders – it was all leading to this: A case too big to ignore. A win too massive to deny.

The Cost at Home

At home, Kimberly laid Joshua gently into his crib, the little boy curling into himself with a soft whimper.

She turned off the bedside lamp and stepped into Sarah's room, where the little girl sat stiffly in her recital dress, violin case untouched at her feet.

"Daddy's working," Kimberly said softly.

Sarah didn't answer.

She didn't cry.

She simply turned away, brushing her hair in slow, deliberate strokes – as if trying to brush the night away.

Kimberly lingered in the doorway, the ache of James's absence pressing heavier with every breath.

She was tired of being the one who stayed.

Tired of telling the children he still loved them, even as love ranked second to ambition.

She was tired of being the only hero left in their home.

Preparing for Battle

Back at Brady & Sanderson, James leaned into the cold glow of his laptop, scrolling through damning evidence:

- Hidden losses.
- Fake valuations.
- Intimidated clients.

Silvermere had built its empire on lies – and now, James would tear it apart.

If he succeeded, the whispers would stop.

If he succeeded, his father would have no choice but to see him – not as a son, but as a successor.

James's fingers tightened around the mouse.

The crown was almost within reach.

And whatever it cost – his wife, his children, even the last shreds of who he used to be – he would take it.

Thursday Morning: Main Conference Room

The partners gathered around the vast mahogany table, murmuring in low, polished voices.

Silver cufflinks glinted. Coffee steamed.

Power lingered like smoke.

At the head of the room, framed by the skyline's jagged teeth, stood James Brady – the founder's son.

No notes.

No slides.

Just a single leather folder resting lightly in his hand.

He looked every inch the senior associate:

- Polished.
- Calm.
- Dangerous.

But under the still surface:

- Hunger.
- Cold rage.
- The electric hum of a man ready to rewrite his destiny.

He wasn't here to inherit the firm.

He was here to take it.

The Pitch

James spoke, voice level:

"Thank you for giving me fifteen minutes."

(A lie, of course – he had forced this meeting.)

He placed the folder on the table with slow, deliberate precision, letting the silence stretch until it tightened around their throats.

Then:

"What if I told you Brady & Sanderson could front the first major private class action of the decade?"

A few heads tilted.

A few sceptical smiles curled.

James pressed on:

"Hundreds of plaintiffs. Clear, documented negligence. A solvent defendant – Silvermere Financial – carrying over fifty million dollars in active insurance."

The name Silvermere floated through the room like a ghost – respected, rich, enmeshed in half the boardrooms in town.

He let it sit there, heavy.

Then:

"And a narrative the media will devour:

Retirees.

Farmers.

Small business owners.

All lied to. All cheated."

The silence that followed wasn't hostile.

It was charged.

The First Challenge

Across the table, Greyson, one of the firm's oldest and most sceptical, non-equity partners, leaned back.

"Expensive," he said lazily.

"And risky."

James smiled, thin and controlled.

He snapped open the folder, revealing neatly stacked financials.

"Already addressed," he said crisply.

"Litigation Risk Liability is prepared to fund up to five million against costs and fees."

He paused, savouring the tiny shift as bodies leaned subtly forward.

"No exposure to Brady & Sanderson.

No risk to the bottom line."

The Turning Point

Harold Sanderson, brilliant and razor-sharp, folded his arms.

"And what's the upside, Brady?"

James slid the next page forward – numbers sharp and deadly as a blade.

"Plaintiff-side contingency: thirty per cent of settlement or judgment."

His voice dropped, magnetic:

"Estimated damages between thirty-five and forty-five million dollars."

Silence fell like a held breath.

"Even if we settle low," he added. "Brady & Sanderson stands to clear twenty to thirty million dollars. Within eighteen months."

No one was smiling now.

They were calculating.

The Crucial Gaze

At the far end of the table, Alexander Brady sat – arms crossed, face carved from stone.

No approval.

No affection.

Just a cold, surgical appraisal.

James met his gaze without blinking.

He wasn't asking for permission.

He wasn't asking for love.

He was offering victory.

And for the first time, James allowed himself a flicker of satisfaction:

Almost there.

Almost king.

Inside Stawell Chambers

Inside Stawell Chambers, the air was thick with the scent of polished wood and old ambition.

James and his team wound their way through narrow corridors, past oil portraits of the great barristers of yesterday, until they reached his barrister's chambers.

A firm knock.

The door creaked open to reveal the barrister, already buried in a sea of legal documents.

"James, gentlemen," the barrister said, waving them in. "Let's strategise before the settlement conference."

They huddled around the antique oak table, sunlight filtering through tall windows.

Maps, charts, and legal briefs sprawled like a battlefield.

Hours passed, sharpening the blade.

Finally, James stood, adjusting his tie, gaze steady.

"Let's proceed," he said.

"Time to make our case."

With legal bags slung over their shoulders, they crossed the street to the looming Supreme Court of Victoria, its columns a testament to tradition – and to the war James intended to win.

Scene: Settlement Conference Room, Supreme Court of Victoria

The atmosphere crackled as both teams settled in.

Across the table, the respondent's barrister – grey-haired, silk-tied, smug – leaned forward.

"Before we proceed, this meeting is conducted on a 'without prejudice' basis?"

James's barrister leaned forward with a faint smirk.

"Of course, my friend. We're here to seek justice, not technicalities."

A ripple of cautious chuckles followed.

James leaned in too, voice calm, lethal.

"Let's focus on finding a resolution that serves everyone.

After all, justice delayed is justice denied."

The First Offer

The respondent's barrister dropped it casually:

"Eighteen million dollars. Full release. No admissions."

James didn't blink.

He let the silence sit. Stretch. Burn.

Behind him, a junior associate shifted uneasily.

Eighteen million wasn't nothing.

Split across hundreds of plaintiffs – funded costs deducted, it was safe.

It was easy.

It was cowardice.

James's Response

James finally leaned in, slow and deliberate.

"No."

The respondent's lawyer arched an eyebrow.

"Mr Brady, eighteen million is a substantial—"

James cut him off, voice cold, precise:

"Forty-two million."

The room froze.

James kept going:

"You defrauded pensioners, farmers, and shopkeepers. You lied on the prospectuses.

You altered customer statements after the market fell. We have the documents. We have your internal emails."

He tapped the unopened, heavy folder on the table.

"If you want to explain that to a jury," James said, smiling faintly, "I welcome it."

The Mediator Intervenes

The mediator coughed politely.

"Perhaps… we should take a short break."

The sides filed out.

In Private (James's Team Room)

Inside their room, a junior associate hissed:

"James, are you sure? Forty-two's… a big jump."

James didn't answer immediately.

He poured a glass of water. Sipped.

Then he said, quiet but absolute:

"Eighteen million buys their comfort. Forty-two million buys their shame. We're not here to make it easy for them."

Silence.

And in that moment, even the hardened litigation funders saw it:

James Brady wasn't playing games anymore.

He wasn't playing anything.

He was building an empire.

The Final Settlement

The air was thick with tension.

James Brady sat at the head of the table, his expression unreadable.

Across from him, Silvermere's lead counsel leaned forward, voice steady:

"Mr Brady, after thorough consideration, Silvermere is prepared to offer thirty-eight point five million dollars to settle this matter."

A hush fell over the room.

James's team exchanged glances, the weight of the number settling in.

James nodded slowly, his voice calm:

"We'll need to review the terms in detail, but that figure is within the realm of reason."

The mediator interjected:

"Shall we reconvene in an hour to finalise the agreement?"

James stood, extending his hand.

The Court's Approval

The courtroom buzzed with anticipation.

James Brady sat at the solicitor's table, posture composed, eyes fixed ahead.

Beside him, his barrister reviewed notes, preparing to address the court.

The presiding judge entered, taking his seat with a nod to the assembled counsel.

Judge: "We are here to consider the application for approval of the proposed settlement in the matter of *Brady v. Silvermere Financial*, pursuant to Section 33V of the Supreme Court Act 1986 (Vic)."

The barrister rose, his voice steady and authoritative.

"Your Honour, the parties have reached a settlement agreement totalling $38.5 million. We submit that this settlement is fair and reasonable, considering the risks and costs associated with proceeding to trial."

The judge nodded, flipping through the documents before him.

Judge: "I note that notices were disseminated to all group members, providing them the opportunity to object or opt out, as required under Section 33X."

"Indeed, Your Honour," the barrister replied. "The notice period concluded with minimal objections, and the majority of group members have expressed satisfaction with the proposed terms."

After a brief deliberation, the judge delivered his decision.

Judge: "Having reviewed the submissions and considered the interests of all group members, the court approves the settlement. The terms are deemed fair and reasonable."

A collective exhale filled the courtroom.

James allowed himself a momentary smile, acknowledging the culmination of months of relentless effort.

The Celebration

The firm's main conference room was transformed, adorned with banners and filled with the buzz of celebration.

Colleagues, investigators, and staff gathered, glasses in hand, to honour the firm's landmark achievement.

As James entered, a wave of applause erupted.

Crowd: "All hail the king!"

James raised his glass, his voice resonating with gratitude and resolve:

James: "This victory is not mine alone. It's a testament to our collective dedication, integrity and pursuit of justice. Here's to many more."

The room echoed with cheers, the celebration continuing into the night.

Maria and John Doors – The Bears Are Just the Beginning

Maria lingered near the old milk fridge, her fingers resting on the door handle that never quite shut properly. She wasn't looking at Kimberly – she was staring into the back of the shop.

"I just thought… maybe we'd hold on. For a bit longer. The kids love it here. Sarah always picks her own fruit like she owns the place. And Joshua, you know him—"

"Thinks it's the best playground in the world," Kimberly said softly. "I know."

Maria smiled, her eyes already wet.

"Last month, your father let him ride in the forklift with him. He wouldn't stop talking about it. Said he could see the whole shopping centre from up there."

"I saw," Kimberly said. "Dad looked so proud."

They stood for a moment in silence, the hum of the centre fading behind the roller door.

Then Kimberly stepped forward – not to argue, but to honour.

"Mum," she said gently, "I'm proud of this shop. You know that. I grew up here. I learned how to work, how to talk to people, and how to think. This place shaped me."

Maria's voice cracked slightly.

"So why are we selling?"

Kimberly took her hands, grounding them both.

"Because I'm proud of you. And Dad. And everything you built. And I'm proud of my children – whether they become grocers or Prime Ministers, I'll be just as proud. But here's the truth…"

She let the words settle before continuing.

"You're sixty-four. Dad's almost seventy. Sarah is nine. Joshua's two. You can't spend the next ten years behind this counter hoping one of them will take it on."

Maria's eyes flickered. "But what if I'm not ready to stop working?"

Kimberly smiled gently.

"Then work – but on your own terms. Do the books for someone else. Bake. Travel. Volunteer. But don't hold on for a future that might never come. Don't wait here, day after day, for a child to grow into your dream."

Maria's voice dropped to a whisper.

"Maybe we could keep it a little longer. Angelo and Brad can manage the floor. The register ladies can help. They're my friends. They've been with us through everything."

Kimberly stepped closer, her voice full of love and care.

"Mum, I know. I love them too. But you and I both know – Angelo and Brad aren't buyers."

Maria looked up, uncertain. Kimberly continued.

"Dad is a buyer. He walks through the market at four in the morning and knows which box of apricots will hold until Sunday and which won't last through Thursday."

"He can read a farmer's handshake. He remembers who paid in full during the drought and who vanished during the floods. That's not just experience – that's instinct. Forty years of it."

"Angelo and Brad are loyal. They're strong. They have good hands and good hearts. And the register ladies – they're the soul of this place. But none of them are buyers."

"They don't walk the rows. They don't choose. They don't know the markets like Dad does. They were never meant to carry that responsibility."

Kimberly took a steady breath.

"I've seen what happens when shops like this are left without a buyer. It doesn't take long – eighteen months, maybe two years. A few overpaid crates. A missed delivery. A deadline slips. Super gets delayed. Rent piles up."

"And then?" She looked straight at her mother.

"Receivership. Creditors. Liquidators. Everything you and Dad built – gone. Not from laziness or malice. Just from the slow weight of the wrong people carrying the right dream."

Maria drew herself up slightly. Her voice had an edge now.

"Kimberly, I can handle this. This is my job."

Then, after a beat – quiet, but cutting:

"Don't you defend people like that poor Michelle Jarr?"

Kimberly didn't flinch. Her reply was calm, clear, and deeply hers.

"I do. And I'm proud of that. I still take Legal Aid cases, Mum. I always will. But that's not all I do."

She took a small step forward, lifting her chin.

"I'm also a commercial litigator. I specialise in mergers and acquisitions. I negotiate multi-million-dollar deals every week."

"I can handle this for you. You don't need a big firm with its expensive fees. I'll do it myself."

She softened her voice.

"I'll get you and Dad a good price – one that honours what you've built. And I'll make it a condition of sale that the staff stay on. Not just Angelo and Brad, but the register ladies too."

"They won't be left behind. No one will."

Maria didn't speak. Her hands, still held in Kimberly's, trembled just slightly.

Kimberly's email that night to work:

To: Compliance Officer – Brady and Sanderson

Subject: Pro Bono Notification – Private Family Matter

Dear Compliance,

I'm advising my parents (John and Maria Doors) in their personal capacity regarding the private sale of their business, Doors Fruit & Veg, located at Brandon Park Shopping Centre.

I will be acting in my capacity as a solicitor (not on behalf of the firm). No firm branding, resources, or staff will be used. The matter is low-risk, non-contentious, and strictly personal.

Please let me know if further disclosure is required.

Regards,

Kimberly Brady

Senior Associate | Commercial Litigation and M&A

Brady & Anderson

She even called her friend from uni – now working at a retail-focused marketing agency – and had a professionally designed advertisement up within seventy-two hours.

"Successful long-standing greengrocer in a vibrant multicultural centre. Excellent community reputation, loyal customer base, and high-yield layout. Includes forklift, cold room, and all existing staff. Turn-key opportunity. Walk in and begin trading."

She refused to list it on a low-rent classifieds site. She went straight to targeted commercial buyers and took three calls within the first day.

Scene: Her Parents Watch in Awe

Her parents stood behind the counter two weeks later, stunned, as Kimberly flipped through five formal expressions of interest, each neatly tabbed and summarised.

"This one's backed by a local grocer with three other outlets – he wants a Monash foothold. Good reputation, good liquidity. This one's a family team – they're new to retail but passionate. And this one" – she smiled – "offered thirty per cent above asking after they saw the Saturday foot traffic figures I provided."

Her mother stared.

"You… you asked for *how much*?"

"Mum, I knew the goodwill in this brand was undervalued. I priced it properly."

The Bears

The night before the sale, Kimberly brought Sarah and Joshua to her parents' house for dinner. After the plates were cleared and the kettle boiled, John reached for his favourite DVD: *Grizzlies of Canada*.

As the screen lit up with sweeping forests and glacial rivers, he leaned forward, speaking to his grandchildren like a nature guide.

"Now watch this," he said, pointing. "See that mother bear? She's not just fishing – she's protecting her cub. Clever girl. Watch how she places herself between him and the current."

Sarah leaned in, wide-eyed. Joshua bounced slightly on the couch, already captivated.

Kimberly watched her father's face – the way he studied the bear, half in admiration, half in longing. And just like that, an idea struck.

She opened her laptop, clicked rapidly through saved links and photos.

Wooden viewing shelters are nestled beside rivers. Guests in puffer jackets holding thermoses. A massive grizzly lumbering into the frame, just metres away.

"Dad," she said, spinning the laptop towards him. "You and Mum are going to Canada."

John blinked.

"To see the bears," she continued. "To see your dream. And now, thanks to the sale… you can afford it."

She tapped on a photo – a man in a folding chair sitting quietly behind a timber screen as a four-hundred-kilo grizzly swiped a salmon out of mid-air.

"You don't even need to hike," she added. "They've built these quiet wooden platforms – raised and reinforced. You sit behind slats or glass. Just watch. No danger. No noise. It's safe."

John squinted at the screen.

"I'm not John West, you know," he said dryly. "I don't want to get eaten for my troubles."

Maria snorted.

Kimberly grinned.

"No wrestling bears, Dad. No canned fish glory. Just you, a camera, and the smartest bear in the river."

John leaned back in his chair, thoughtful.

"All right," he said finally. "As long as the bear doesn't want me for dinner."

"She's got salmon," Kimberly replied. "You're safe."

The deal was signed on-site. Kimberly brought the documents, and the new owners brought pastries. The employees were introduced with handshakes and smiles.

"You'll all be staying on," Kimberly said clearly, in front of everyone. "No changes to hours, rates, or rosters unless you agree to them."

The staff – mostly migrants, casuals, part-timers – nodded with quiet relief. One of them teared up.

Her father, who had been quiet for most of the process, finally spoke as they were locking up.

"I didn't think it would end like this. But it ended well. That matters."

Kimberly smiled, tired but proud.

"It didn't end. It transitioned."

Nicholas Brady – Little One, Quiet Voice

She pushed through her discomfort with the sort of poise that had long defined her – a calm forged in cross-examinations and custody hearings and early-morning sentencing reports. But the body has a way of insisting.

By midday, Kimberly hadn't returned from her office. A clerk knocked once, gently, then again with urgency. When the door opened, she was seated at her desk, elbows resting on her files, hands clutching the arms of her chair. She was pale. Sweating. Her eyes glazed with a sort of quiet panic that didn't suit someone like her – someone who had stood eye to eye with Supreme Court justices and never once blinked first.

Jill rushed in, followed by Carson and two junior clerks. Kimberly tried to stand, instinctively – the leader, the mentor, the name on the door – but the moment she moved, a sharp cramp stole her words and bent her forward.

"Call an ambulance," Jill ordered, without hesitation.

And so they did.

Within moments, the office that had long prided itself on decorum and pace was suspended in chaos – the wrong kind of silence. Associates stood frozen, watching the paramedics enter in neon yellow, wheeling the gurney toward her glass-walled office.

Kimberly lifted her chin as they approached, though her skin was now ashen and clammy. Her eyes flicked to the diploma above her desk – Monash Law, First Class Honours – and then to the photograph beside it, of Sarah and Joshua, arms slung over one another, mid-laugh.

"She's thirty weeks," one paramedic said. "Vitals are dropping. Let's go."

No one asked her who to call. They already knew. Not James. Not the board. Not the press.

Harold Sanderson stepped out of his office just in time to see her being wheeled past. For the first time in thirty years, he was visibly rattled. He reached for her hand, but she was already fading into the noise of sirens and hallway chatter.

At the Royal Women's Hospital, they cleared a bay for her.

Outside, rain tapped on the windows. Inside, a monitor beeped in rhythms that seemed too fast, then too slow. Nurses whispered. Midwives moved quickly. A specialist came in, then another.

Kimberly Brady, fierce defender of the bench, advocate for the broken and principled to her bones, was now just a woman. A mother. A body in a gown, hands on her stomach, whispering to the child within.

"Stay. Please stay."

The room was a controlled hum – machines blinking in green and amber, oxygen monitors gently ticking, the distant roll of a trolley echoing from the corridor.

Kimberly shifted against the pillows, her gown loose across her shoulders, her breath steadier now but thin. James sat beside her, still in his court shoes, silent, holding her hand with the quiet determination of someone trying not to make anything worse.

Then came the knock.

The door opened, and in stepped a tall, elegant man in his mid-fifties, grey at the temples but with the energy of someone much younger. He wore a charcoal wool suit beneath his white coat –

bespoke, but modest. His name tag read Dr Elias Patrinos – her private obstetrician and gynaecologist.

He had been with her through both previous pregnancies. A man of calm precision, British like her mother, always knowing exactly when to speak, and when to simply let a mother listen to her body.

"Kimberly," he said, with a nod of genuine warmth, "You called me in early this morning. I left my surgery immediately. You're in the right place now."

Behind him followed a younger woman in scrubs – her manner observant, quiet, but confident. She carried a tablet and wore a small gold cross on a chain beneath her ID badge.

"This is Dr Leila Nader," Dr Patrinos continued. "She's a colleague of mine – a perinatal specialist and neonatologist. I'll be looking after you. Dr Nader is here for your baby."

Kimberly blinked slowly, processing the subtle yet profound meaning.

"You're both staying?" she asked, her voice no louder than a breath.

Dr Patrinos stepped to her side, placing two fingers gently on her wrist – not to take her pulse, but as reassurance. "You're a private patient, Kimberly. We have privileges here, and you have priority. We're staying."

He glanced at the monitor. "I've reviewed the contractions. Mild uterine irritability, nothing consistent yet. Your cervix is closed, which is good. We're not in labour – but this was a warning shot. And we listen to those."

Dr Nader nodded. "The baby's doing well for thirty weeks. Strong baseline, reactive trace. But if we need to intervene, we will. I've ordered antenatal corticosteroids for lung maturity and magnesium for neuroprotection."

"I know what that means," Kimberly murmured, her mind half in law and half in medicine. "You're building a runway. In case the baby needs to come early."

"Exactly," Dr Nader replied. "But we're going to try to keep the baby in flight for a few more weeks, if we can. One day at a time."

James stood, grateful but rattled. "And the bleeding? There was spotting earlier."

"Minimal," Dr Patrinos replied. "No placental abruption, no previa. Baby's fluid levels are fine. This isn't an emergency – but it is a line in the sand. From here on out, it's rest. No chambers. No hearings. No late-night briefings, Kimberly. Not even a phone call unless it's to sing lullabies."

The blinds were drawn now. Daylight had softened into a grey wash of filtered afternoon. In the maternity high-dependency unit, the hum of the fetal monitor was steady – but so was the unease curling in Kimberly's chest.

She knew something had changed when Dr Elias Patrinos returned with a tablet in hand and Dr Leila Nader just behind him, now wearing a surgical cap loosely tied at the nape of her neck.

James stood immediately, sensing it too.

Dr Patrinos did not sit. He took a moment, his pause deliberate – the kind of silence that precedes a hard truth spoken with care.

"Kimberly," he began, voice low and steady, "we've monitored everything closely over the last few hours. The uterine irritability has escalated. The fetal heart tracing is becoming less reassuring – subtle decelerations we don't ignore. And your blood pressure has risen steadily, even with rest."

Kimberly shifted against the pillows, her hand instinctively resting over her belly. "But I'm only thirty weeks…"

"You are," he nodded gently. "And I wouldn't be saying this if we had a better option. But we need to introduce your baby early. Today. Possibly within the next few hours."

James sank back into the chair beside the bed, his hands gripping the edge of the armrest.

Dr Patrinos continued, "This isn't a choice we make lightly. But it is the best decision for you both. You're showing signs of early preeclampsia with fetal compromise. If we wait, we risk a severe event – for you and for the baby."

He placed the tablet down, showing a CTG scan. "We'll proceed with a controlled delivery, most likely a caesarean. You'll be fully awake, and we'll be with you every moment."

Kimberly's voice was barely audible. "Will my baby be okay?"

It was Dr Nader who stepped forward now, her tone confident, every word anchored in experience.

"We have the NICU team on standby here at the Royal Women's," she said. "And as soon as your baby is stabilised – which will happen within minutes – we'll transfer them to the Neonatal Intensive Care Unit at the Royal Children's Hospital."

"You won't be alone in this, Kimberly," she added. "You'll see your child before transfer. Our team will handle everything – intubation if needed, temperature regulation, neonatal surfactant, and early respiratory support. It's all in motion."

Kimberly turned her head to James, searching his face not for approval – but for courage.

His voice cracked when he finally spoke. "I'll go with the baby."

She nodded. Of course, he would. He'd never stopped being their father.

Dr Patrinos gently placed a hand on her wrist. "You've been brilliant, Kimberly. Fierce. Graceful. But now… it's time to hand the baton to us. Let us run this next part."

Kimberly blinked back tears, her lawyer's mind resisting every loss of control. But the mother in her – the woman lying here, fragile and afraid – nodded once.

"Okay," she whispered. "Let's do it."

Dr Nader turned to the nurse behind her and gave a single nod.

"Prepping for theatre. Let's bring this little one safely into the world."

The theatre lights were sterile and bright. Kimberly lay still on the operating table, the drape shielding her view, her body numb from the spinal block, but her mind sharp – counting every second.

She heard it before she felt it: the cry.

It was thin, uncertain – like a violin string drawn too tight – but it was there. And it shattered the tension in the room.

"Nicholas," she whispered. The name they had chosen but hadn't spoken aloud until now. "That's his name."

Dr Nader smiled behind her mask, nodding to the neonatal team. "Baby Nicholas Brady. Born 1.6 kilograms. He's breathing. He's with us."

The NICU team swarmed gently, expertly. One nurse wrapped the baby in a warmed towel; another attached the pulse ox monitor. The neonatologist – calm, efficient – checked reflexes, gave the all-clear to initiate transfer protocols.

But before they moved him, before the world could pull her child into another ward, Kimberly spoke.

"Let me see him."

And they did.

A nurse brought Nicholas over, the bundle small and trembling, like a fledgling bird. His skin was dusky pink, his eyes sealed shut, his fists clenched as if he were already trying to hold on.

Kimberly reached out with one hand – trembling from the drugs, from the adrenaline, from the awe – and touched his cheek.

"Hi, baby boy," she whispered. "You're early, but you're everything."

She pressed her lips to his forehead – a feather of a kiss – and the moment sealed into her forever.

Then, as quickly as it came, the moment passed.

"We need to go now," the neonatologist said gently. "He'll be transferred to the Royal Children's NICU within the hour. We'll update you every step of the way."

They wheeled him out in a temperature-controlled pod, with James following closely behind, silent but fierce in his determination.

And suddenly, she was alone.

Not just in the recovery room, but in the aching space between mother and child. Between body and breath. Between the echo of that first cry and the next time she'd hear it again.

No monitors to listen for. No tiny chest rising beside her.

Just white walls. A folded blanket. The silence of separation.

Her arms were empty. Her son – a floor away, then a wing, then another hospital entirely. And no amount of legal training could teach her how to feel that.

A nurse checked her vitals. Another adjusted the IV. Kimberly turned her head to the window and let the tears come silently. Not out of fear. Not out of grief.

But out of love. And the cost of surviving.

The Space Between Us

A week after the operation, Kimberly was discharged from the Royal Women's Hospital.

There was no fanfare, no celebration. Just a nurse placing her belongings in a white hospital bag and handing her a folder of discharge papers. Her belly was still sore, her breasts full, but there was no baby to carry with her. No car seat. No bundle of joy.

Only silence.

She left the hospital holding a breast pump and a tube of lanolin cream. Her arms felt too light. Her heart is too heavy.

James drove her home to Brighton, where her mother had folded the laundry and her father had made dinner for the kids. Sarah and Josh ran to the door, hugging her around the waist, careful not to press too hard against the scar beneath her clothes.

"Nicholas?" Sarah whispered.

"He's still at the Children's," Kimberly answered softly. "Mummy will be with him tomorrow. Every day."

And she was.

From that morning forward, Nicholas Brady's world began and ended in a glass box – warm, sterile, cocooned inside the humming NICU ward at the Royal Children's Hospital. Kimberly would arrive early, just after the school drop-off. She'd sit for hours with her palm resting gently against the isolette, her milk labelled in bags and handed to the nurses, her body present even when her baby could not feed from her directly.

She sang lullabies. Read from books. Whispered stories about the courtroom and about his brother and sister, who hadn't met him yet – not yet.

The hospital had become her church. Her courtroom. Her only rhythm.

At first, James tried. He brought her coffee. Sat by the isolette for twenty minutes here, an hour there. He helped at home –

cooked for the kids, paid the bills, filled out forms. He didn't complain.

But slowly, without notice, he stopped meeting her eyes. His back grew tighter. His jaw clenched more often. His voice, still polite, was now clipped at the ends.

Her parents had moved into their old guest room. Her mother folded the school uniforms. Her father drove Sarah to her violin lesson. Their lives took over his house – not rudely, not loudly – but completely.

One night, after a late pump session at two a.m., Kimberly came home and found James asleep on the couch. Not drunk. Not angry. Just tired. He didn't stir when she passed. He barely moved when she slipped into the bedroom to cry alone.

Autumn Turned to Winter

Nicholas reached thirty-six weeks, still growing slowly. He had chronic lung issues, a weak suck reflex. He'd coded once – blue, terrifying – and had to be bagged and revived in front of Kimberly. That day, she stopped sleeping altogether. From then on, she sat by his side until the lights dimmed and the shift nurses insisted she go home.

James was there the night Nicholas first opened his eyes. Kimberly called him, breathless. "Come now, he's looking around."

James came. He smiled. He stood beside her, resting his hand gently on her shoulder.

But he didn't cry.

And Kimberly did.

What Was Meant to Heal Them Didn't

Their son was supposed to be the thread. The repair. The reminder of how strong they'd once been.

But the daily dividing line – her with Nicholas, him with everything else – grew too wide.

James began working late.

Kimberly stopped asking why.

They didn't fight.

There was no betrayal. No raised voices. No slammed doors.

Just a quiet resignation. A marriage softly curling in on itself – like a sheet of paper burning slowly from the edge, the centre still intact but already lost.

Home but without

Nicholas finally came home at five months old.

He weighed less than a watermelon.

The first night, Kimberly slept in the nursery beside him, her hand resting on the crib.

James slept in the other room. "Just for now," he'd said. "Just while your parents are still here."

But now never ended.

The house was full – of people, noise, and the sound of machines keeping a fragile boy breathing – but Kimberly had never felt so alone.

She had saved her son.

But somewhere along the way, she had lost her husband.

Kimberly Brady – Her Honour's Path

James Brady hadn't just inherited a seat at the table. He had started clearing the table entirely.

When his father, Alexander Brady, retired from the firm, he handed James his full equity stake. It was meant to be a legacy gift, a continuation of the Brady name. But James saw it for what it was: leverage.

The moment Harold Sanderson announced his own retirement, James made his move. Rather than allow the firm to promote one of the waiting senior associates, James offered to purchase Harold's equity stake outright.

He didn't need the money. He had the collateral. Alexander's equity was fully paid. James used it to secure the loan, signed his name personally, and took full ownership of not just one partner seat – but two.

The managing committee barely had time to blink. There were no objections. James was, after all, the golden boy with the class action win. The man with headlines, clients and prestige.

The senior associates watched their dreams of equity evaporate overnight. Kimberly watched in silence.

She had expected politics. She hadn't expected a full consolidation.

It became clear to everyone that James didn't want partners. He wanted control. What once had been a firm built on collaboration was now a silent boardroom with one voice that echoed twice as loud.

She walked past his office that afternoon. Floor-to-ceiling windows. The city skyline shimmered behind him. He didn't see her. Or maybe he did, and chose not to.

She didn't stop.

The day Harold Sanderson said goodbye, Kimberly Brady quietly stepped away from the life she thought she was meant to build.

Harold had packed up his office without ceremony. No champagne, no farewell dinner, just a quiet calendar note and a few boxes marked in his own neat handwriting. But before he left the building for the last time, he asked Kimberly to meet him in the courtyard. Not in the boardroom, not in chambers. Just the garden behind the sandstone walls where the firm had grown around them both.

She arrived to find him seated on the stone bench, an envelope resting in his lap. He stood as she approached and handed it to her with the care of a man placing something sacred into safe hands.

"I didn't say anything in the partner meeting," he began. "Not the right room for this. But I wanted you to have this before I left."

Kimberly opened the envelope. The moment her eyes found the first line, her breath caught.

To the Judicial Appointments Advisory Panel…

She read on in silence. It was a nomination. A full judicial endorsement for a seat on the County Court bench. Written not with flattery, but with clarity, honesty, and conviction. Harold had detailed her courtroom work, her leadership, her ethics. He had seen what she had hoped someone would see all along.

When she looked up, her voice was small. "You're recommending me for the bench?"

He nodded. "Not just recommending. I've spoken to people. The panel knows your name. They respect your work. They're watching."

She shook her head, still stunned. "I thought I had to prove something here first. Equity. Recognition. I thought I had to win my way through James."

Harold's smile was thin, but kind. "You shouldn't have stayed this long. Not here. And don't go looking for an associate position somewhere else. A brilliant legal mind like yours doesn't need to play small to survive."

He stepped back and looked at the sky over the rooftops. "James is consolidating, not collaborating. He doesn't want partners. He wants control. And while you could fight him and probably win, you'd bleed for every inch. That's not legacy. That's noise."

She was quiet for a long time. Then she said, almost without breath, "I believed I could still do good from inside."

"You did," he said. "Now go do something greater."

She took a step forward and embraced him. It wasn't dramatic. It wasn't performative. Just two people sharing a moment of truth. He held her gently, as a father might, not with possession, but with pride.

When she stepped back, her eyes were glassy. "Thank you, Harold."

Harold took a small step away and, with a dignified nod, bowed his head.

"It's my honour… Your Honour."

End of Part Two

Part III – Her Honourable Justice Kimberly Judith Brady

Justice Brady – Robing Ceremony

County Court of Victoria – Courtroom 3.2

Monday Morning, ten a.m.

Courtroom 3.2 wasn't as grand as those in the Supreme Court, but it carried a different weight – a lived-in authority. The kind of courtroom where real people argued real cases and hard decisions were made every day. It was, in many ways, the perfect place for Kimberly Brady's swearing-in.

The gallery filled early. Court staff brought in extra chairs. The air hummed with whispered conversations, shuffling robes, and the faint scent of coffee brought in by someone who didn't know better.

The seats reserved for James Brady & Associates were nearly all occupied. Former partners, current associates – even Beverly Harrington, the long-time office manager turned close friend and ally, had come. She still maintained her rule: every coffee cup must have a lid.

A few attendees glanced around, exchanging quiet, knowing looks: both James Brady and his father were conspicuously absent.

But someone even more significant was there.

Harold Sanderson, sitting with former staff, sat silently in the second row, just behind the press. No announcement, no fuss – just Harold. Present. Watching.

Front Row: The Doors Family

Front and centre, where it mattered most, sat John and Marie Doors, their posture dignified, their faces aglow. Marie had baby Nicholas nestled gently in her arms, wrapped in a white blanket she'd knitted herself. He was asleep, head resting near the string of pearls she always wore for special occasions.

Beside them, Joshua – three years old, swinging his legs and holding a half-unwrapped chocolate – and Sarah, calm and composed, wearing her Mentone Girls' Grammar uniform. In her lap, she clutched a small card with 'For Mum' written in lavender marker and stick-on stars.

Marie leaned over to her granddaughter.

"She's coming in now, love. Look sharp."

Kimberly Enters

As the usher called the courtroom to order, Kimberly stepped into view.

She wore her new judicial robes – fitted to perfection, crisp and heavy with meaning. But even more striking than her attire was her poise. Calm. Steady. Proud.

She scanned the courtroom only once – pausing briefly when her eyes found Harold, and then again when they landed on her parents. Her mother smiled softly, gently rocking Nicholas. Her father's eyes shone.

The Oath

The Presiding Judge administered the oath. Kimberly raised her right hand, her voice clear and sure:

"I, Kimberly Judith Brady, do swear that I will well and truly serve the people of Victoria in the office of Judge of the County Court, and I will do right to all manner of people according to law, without fear or favour, affection or ill-will. So help me God."

There was no thunderous applause – this was the County Court – but there was a respectful ripple, the kind that runs through seasoned professionals who know what this moment really means.

Judicial Remarks

The Presiding Judge offered remarks that were both formal and warm:

Judge Brady has built her career on substance – not posturing. In addition to her work in commercial litigation, she undertook pro bono representation through Legal Aid in family violence and criminal matters, demonstrating her commitment to access to justice. She has earned the respect of both the bench and the bar. Her appointment strengthens this Court.

He paused, smiling slightly as he gestured toward the packed rows behind her.

"And when a courtroom fills like this – from chambers to clerks to retired judges – it speaks volumes about the woman being sworn."

Kimberly's Speech

Kimberly took the lectern. She looked confident – but her voice softened the moment she spoke:

"This is not just a professional milestone. For me, this is personal."

"To my colleagues at James Brady & Associates – thank you. You challenged me, taught me, and made me believe that I belonged in this profession, even when it didn't always feel like I did."

There was a long pause.

"To Harold Sanderson – your presence here today moves me deeply. You showed me what a just courtroom feels like. And I carry that lesson with me."

She turned to her family.

“To Mum and Dad – who woke me up at three a.m. to head to the markets, and taught me to think on my feet and speak with respect. To Sarah – who inspires me every day with her clarity and compassion. To Joshua, who keeps me laughing. And to baby Nicholas – held by the same arms that first held me…”

Her voice caught, just for a moment.

“This robe is heavy. But your love makes it feel light.”

After the Ceremony

Outside the courtroom, in the bright atrium of the County Court, people gathered for hugs, photos and polite congratulations.

John Doors shook hands like a proud father at a wedding. Marie received compliments on the baby – and her blanket. Sarah handed Kimberly the card, then whispered, “You didn’t cry. I thought you might.”

Kimberly grinned. “Almost.”

Then, from the shadows of the atrium, Harold Sanderson approached. He didn’t say much. Just took her hand in both of his and said:

“You’ll be good for this place.”

“Thank you, Harold.”

He gave Sarah a small nod, tipped his head to Marie, and disappeared through the glass doors like the quiet elder statesman he was.

Scene: The Photograph

The robing room was quieter than usual.

It had been a long morning – ceremonial, official, and filled with speeches from peers who knew only fragments of the story. Kimberly had sat for the formal portraits already, alone in full judicial robes. But this one – this one was hers. The only one she had truly asked for.

The door creaked open, and Sarah walked in first, her white stockings peeking out beneath her jarrah-coloured skirt, her red blazer buttoned neatly over her shirt. She was ten now – graceful already in the way she held her hands and stood with her shoulders back. The way she looked at her mother in the red sash and wig – it was more than pride. It was knowing. A quiet recognition passed between them, unspoken but deeply felt.

Kimberly knelt slightly, adjusting her robes and steadying her footing as her mother gently passed baby Nicholas into her arms. His fingers curled instinctively around the fabric of her collar, and he nestled into her shoulder, soft and warm. Kimberly breathed him in – the powder, the milk, the unmistakable scent of new life. He made no sound, only settled.

Joshua toddled in a step behind, clutching a worn little toy truck in one hand and dragging his feet as if uncertain whether he belonged in a room like this. Kimberly reached out with her free hand and guided him in, pulling him gently toward her leg.

"Come, darling," she whispered. "Stay close."

The photographer adjusted his lighting, then paused. "May I?"

Kimberly nodded, already shifting her weight to balance Nicholas and bring her children around her. Joshua leaned into her robes at thigh-height, his cheek pressing into the heavy crimson. Sarah stood slightly to the side, upright, still, composed – but her hand found Joshua's, and held it.

The photographer took a breath, then clicked.

Flash.

It was the photograph chosen for the *Law Review* Magazine, and later displayed in the grand hallway of Melbourne University's Law School – the one her daughter, Sarah, would one day pass on her way to the library, perhaps without a word, but not without feeling.

Yet it hung not only in institutions, but in the hallway of their home – beside the piano, beneath the family calendar filled with music lessons and quiet reminders.

In the frame: the judicial robe, the crimson sash, the solemnity of office. But more than that – beneath the fabric, within the frame – was the woman herself.

A judge, yes. But a mother first.

Holding a newborn in her arms. A toddler wrapped around her legs.

And a daughter – upright, steady – her hand clasped proudly in her little brother's.

Kimberly blinked slowly as the shutter clicked again. She felt the ache behind her eyes but held it. This wasn't just a portrait. It was a record. A testimony.

She stood at the intersection of justice and motherhood, and this photo captured it – not as a contradiction, but as truth.

Nicholas stirred lightly and sighed.

And still, even in his sleep, his tiny hand held the edge of her robe.

Theo Apostolopoulos – You're Going to Gaol

The kettle had boiled ten minutes ago, but no one had poured the tea. The mugs sat, waiting – three of them, mismatched, chipped in places – like they belonged to different households that somehow found themselves at the same table.

Helena sat closest to the window, fingers wrapped loosely around the handle of the kettle, but she hadn't moved. Paul stood by the toaster, not because he wanted toast but because it gave him something to look at. Theo sat across from them both, arms crossed, shoulders hunched, his gaze fixed on a small crack in the kitchen tile floor.

He was thirty-five now. Divorced. Living back with his mother. He'd been there nearly a year.

"I'll pour it," Paul said at last, gently reaching past Helena.

"I was going to," she replied softly, without moving.

Paul took a sip from his own mug.

He stayed behind in the kitchen. The kettle was cold now, the mugs mostly untouched.

He reached for the manila folder resting on the table's edge – the brief of evidence.

It opened with a soft crack. Pages creaked as he turned them, one by one.

Theo would've received a copy too. Whether he'd read it or not was unclear.

Paul flipped past the cover sheet, the charge summary, and the inventory of the engines. Twenty crates. Serial numbers still attached. Warehouse under a lapsed lease. One security camera caught a registration plate. The key was found in Theo's jacket. And the statement from the arresting officer – clinical, precise.

He paused on the witness list. Names he didn't recognise. Names Theo hadn't mentioned.

Paul reached for a pen, marking margins the way he always did – tight comments, little arrows, asterisks. He circled the photo reference: Crate No. 7 – seal broken. That detail hadn't come up in court.

He sat back. The brief didn't lie. But it didn't tell everything either.

Theo reappeared in the doorway, arms folded.

Paul looked up. There was no ceremony in his voice, no attempt to soften the blow.

"You're going to gaol."

Theo didn't blink. "I know."

Paul slid the file closed. "I don't say that to wound you. I say it because you need to know what comes next."

Theo nodded once. "I do."

Paul leaned forward, elbows resting on the table. "You've already pleaded guilty. There's no room to argue the facts. No defence we could mount would hold."

Theo didn't speak.

Paul continued, quietly but firmly. "The prosecution will push for six or seven years. That's the range. We might bring it down with remorse, background, clean record – but it won't disappear."

County Court of Victoria – Courtroom 3

Theo sat silently in the dock, dressed in a collared shirt that Helena had ironed the night before. His hair was neater than usual, his posture stiff but not slouched. He didn't look back.

Paul stood, file in hand, facing the bench. Judge Kimberly Brady sat high above him, her expression composed, the robes framing her like a shoreline around stone.

Helena sat beside her mother three rows back in the public gallery. Her handbag was at her feet. Her hands folded – not in prayer, but in strength.

Paul cleared his throat once, softly.

"The charge before the court is serious," he began, the weight of it unmistakable. "My client was found in possession of twenty high-performance car engines. All were factory-stamped. VIN numbers matched precisely to an automotive racing facility in Sydney. The value is high. The circumstances damning. And the Crown is correct to pursue this with seriousness."

"Your Honour, my client has pleaded guilty at the earliest opportunity. He does not dispute the facts, nor does he seek to diminish the seriousness of the offence. What he asks for today is not leniency, but understanding."

He paused, not for effect, but for breath.

"Theo grew up in a house that never locked its doors. His mother – who is present – taught him what fairness looked like long before any legal textbook tried to explain it, and somewhere along the way, he forgot that. Or more truthfully, he let someone else convince him that fairness was a luxury he couldn't afford."

Kimberly listened without movement. To anyone else in the gallery, she appeared a still figure of legal authority.

But Paul knew her better now – these irregular encounters had taught him that.

He could see the way her gaze never wavered, how her posture held deliberately firm.

She wasn't just listening to the facts.

She was listening to the tone.

And to the man delivering them.

"He is thirty-five. Divorced. A man rebuilding not just reputation, but self. His decision to cooperate, to plead early, to make no excuses – these are not tactics. They are acts of a man who has begun the slow, painful work of owning what he broke."

Helena looked straight ahead.

"This is not a case of a career criminal. This is not a syndicate mastermind. This is a man who made himself useful to people who never once intended to carry his weight. And when it came time to answer for it, they vanished – and he stayed."

Paul held the bench with his eyes.

"He does not come to this court asking for mercy. He comes asking that you see what remains – and not just what was lost."

A long pause. Then:

"Thank you, Your Honour."

He sat down slowly.

The Crown rose.

"Your Honour," the prosecutor began, her tone even, deliberate, "this is a high-value offence involving the possession of twenty stolen high-performance engines with clear ties to a racing facility in New South Wales. The evidence is strong, the VIN matches indisputably, and the logistics of storage indicate organisation beyond a spontaneous act."

She turned a page.

"The Crown acknowledges the early plea and lack of prior convictions. However, the volume of goods and the commercial value, alongside Mr Avery's client's custodial responsibility over the premises and keys, place him in a position of direct culpability."

She looked up at the bench.

"We submit that a sentence in the range of six to seven years would be appropriate in reflecting the seriousness of the offending, maintaining parity with other recent decisions, and ensuring adequate general deterrence."

She sat down.

Judge Brady looked down at the bench papers, then lifted her eyes.

"Theodore Stephanos Apostolopoulos, please rise."

Theo stood, shoulders squared, jaw set.

"You have pleaded guilty to possessing stolen automotive equipment tied to a racing facility interstate. The volume, value, and your control of the warehouse render this a serious offence."

She paused.

"The court acknowledges your early plea, clean record, and the personal circumstances put forward by your counsel. While you were not the architect of this operation, your involvement was not peripheral. You held keys. You were trusted with control. And that trust was breached."

Another pause.

"This sentence must reflect the scale of the offending, the need for deterrence, and the integrity of the justice system."

Kimberly looked directly at him.

"You are sentenced to three years' imprisonment. You will be eligible for parole after serving eighteen months."

She nodded once. "You may be seated."

Theo sat without looking back.

A court officer moved quietly to the side of the dock. No handcuffs. Just a hand on the shoulder. Theo stood again when prompted.

Paul leaned slightly toward him, low enough not to be heard by the court. "We're here for you," he said.

Theo didn't answer. But before turning to follow the officer through the secure door, he looked up – past Paul, beyond the courtroom – to the public gallery.

His eyes found Helena. And beside her, his mother.

He nodded once. Not to explain. Not to apologise. Just to say: I see you.

Then he was gone.

County Court of Victoria – Hallway Outside Courtroom 3

The heavy door thudded shut behind them, sealing the courtroom and its verdict away. The sentence had been clear: three years. No suspended term. No parole eligibility for eighteen months. Theo had nodded once, jaw tight, before being led out the side door. Kimberly Brady remained at the bench, stoic and composed.

Outside, in the marble-floored hallway, Helena stood near one of the long frosted windows, arms folded tightly across her chest.

Her brother was gone now – taken quietly, without a backward glance.

She hadn't come for him. Not really. Not even for the process.

She had come for Paul.

He leaned against the opposite wall, eyes closed, shoulders drawn – the kind of tired that has nothing to do with sleep.

When the courtroom door opened again, it was Judge Brady who stepped through, still in her robes. Her gaze scanned the hallway and landed on Helena. She paused. Then walked over.

Paul straightened instinctively. "Your Honour."

"Mr Avery." Her voice was neutral, but soft.

Helena turned. Kimberly nodded to her – respectful, not warm, but not cold either.

Then something unusual happened. Kimberly Brady gave a short, deliberate nod toward Helena – not a bow, not a judicial inclination, but something like a salute. A small offering. A mark of respect, of parity.

"Mrs Avery," she said.

Helena was momentarily stunned.

This woman – who had just sentenced her husband's client, her brother, to three years – stood before her not with power, but with deference.

Kimberly continued, "He argued with strength and decency. I hope you told him that."

Helena nodded. "I do. Every time."

A beat passed.

"The law can't always offer comfort," Kimberly said. "But it can still try to deliver clarity."

Then she turned to Paul. "He was lucky to have you."

Paul gave a quiet thanks.

There was a stillness now. The kind that settled in after the engines stopped. Kimberly's voice, softer than before, seemed to echo from a different place.

"There are days," she said, "when I feel like the officer in the wardroom, offering the doctor a brandy. He's the one doing the surgery. I'm just trying to keep the lights steady."

Paul blinked. It was the closest thing to vulnerability he'd ever heard from her.

Kimberly met Helena's eyes again, just once more. Then moved past them both, walking down the hall with calm, even steps.

Helena watched her go.

Paul murmured, almost to himself, "She saluted you."

Helena glanced sideways. "Then she sees the cost, too."

It was the first and final time the two women would meet.

Neither said anything more. The hallway held them in stillness until the courthouse echo swallowed the last of Kimberly's footsteps.

Outside, the wind picked up across William Street. Inside, the weight of justice lingered on their shoulders – not as a burden, but as a bond.

Author's Note

Phillip E Carroll

I know this isn't what a judge would do. But I left it in deliberately.

This is the only time in the entire novel that Kimberly and Helena meet.

I couldn't leave it in silence.

In the 1942 film In Which We Serve, Captain Kinross would not – by the book – have saluted the wife of Able Seaman 'Shorty' Blake. But he did. Quietly. Because it was the only true thing to do.

That moment stayed with me.

This is my version of that gesture. A small act of recognition.

Not judicial – but human.

A bow to emotional truth.

A salute to Noël Coward – whose wit and restraint echo across this book, from the dinner tables to the dock.

Helena Avery – Light That Does Not Go Out

By the time Holy Week arrived, Paul had settled into a rhythm at work that was steady and deeply respected. His practice at Franks & Valentine's Broadmeadows office had grown not just in caseload, but in quiet reputation. He was the man people came to when things truly mattered – tenancy disputes, intervention orders, youth justice pleas that needed more than just a legal argument. He never raised his voice in court. He didn't need to. Judges listened. Clients returned. His calendar filled itself.

He handled most of his matters between Broadmeadows and Sunshine, occasionally taking the train into the city for a Melbourne appearance. But Broadmeadows was home base – the working end of the Franks' legal machine, where the cases never stopped and the community never let go.

Paul liked it that way. He didn't need glass offices or corner views. He needed clarity, good coffee, and a team that trusted him. And that, he had.

The salary – $110,000 a year to bring in a top earner for the patch – was more than Paul could refuse. They wanted his knowledge, his instincts, his name known at the Broadmeadows registry.

Helena was happy. The mortgage was manageable now. No more stress at the letterbox. No more late-night sums at the kitchen table. They could breathe.

Paul could give his family the comfort they deserved – not luxury, but reliability. A steady home. A garden. A life where things didn't fall apart every time the car needed a service.

That was the life he chose. And quietly, steadily, it fit.

Paul Avery finished higher than David Franks at Melbourne Uni. Made less than James. And smiled more than either of them. That was enough.

The only event the firm ever truly expected him to attend was the annual Franks & Valentine Christmas Picnic. Held just before the courts closed for summer, it was an oddly formal affair masquerading as casual – partners in linen suits, associates in carefully relaxed polos, and children running amok with Santa hats and icy poles.

Paul had never cared for office parties. But the picnic? That was different. Helena and the boys came every year, their presence grounding the event in something real. He remembered the year his boys beat the Frank children in the egg-and-spoon race – Helena cheering louder than anyone, her laugh echoing through the gums.

Santa Claus and his helper always handed out gifts that were impossibly perfect – age-appropriate, thoughtful, tailored like someone had done real homework. And they had. Someone in operations, it was rumoured, kept a spreadsheet that was updated more meticulously than case law.

Allegra Preston, always elegant, even at a picnic, wore flowing cotton dresses and wide-brimmed hats as if the event were a Vogue feature. And yet, somehow, she never seemed out of place – just elevated.

Helena would chat warmly with the other spouses, bring a tray of koulourakia wrapped in Christmas paper, and kiss Paul on the cheek when no one was looking.

Paul used to say the picnic was team bonding at its best – and its worst. But that year, as Helena looped her arm through his, he had looked out at the long tables, the laughter, the white gift bags tucked under folding chairs, and thought, *This, too, is part of it.*

At home, Helena was preparing for Easter.

Palm Sunday at East Keilor Parish always began with the same rhythm. Helena would smooth down the boys' shirts, adjust Paul's collar with a familiar tug, and quietly remind them, "Fish only today. You know the rules." Church was solemn, beautiful, packed with families and older women in black. The psalms were sung slowly. The air smelled of incense and fresh lemons from the garden hedge outside.

After liturgy, the community lunch spread out across the hall like a village banquet. Helena's mother was, as always, in command of the kitchen. She was one of 'the Girls' – women who didn't just help at church but made it their life's work. She shouted over boiling pots and gently scolded volunteers for under-seasoning the salad. The tables were full of fried fish, Greek salad, crusty bread, and the gentle hum of memory.

Then came the Easter raffle and the alcohol auction. Paul smiled as Helena handed him her mother's bidding paddle. "Just one bottle," she whispered. That year, Paul paid eighty dollars for a bottle of ouzo he could've gotten for thirty-five dollars at the bottle shop. But that wasn't the point. The point was lifting the paddle. Being seen. Participating.

On Good Friday night, they returned to East Keilor for the candlelit procession. Inside the church, the air was thick with silence and reverence. The Avery family was there, as they always were. Helena gently took Christopher's hand and helped light his candle. When it blew out, she relit her boys' candle with a kiss on the cheek.

Paul stood in awe, the sea of flickering flames tracing a path behind the priest around the block. Children held candles bigger than their hands. Helena's face glowed in the soft light. She carried her flame like it was sacred. And it was.

Midnight liturgy on Holy Saturday brought the climax. The church was packed, unlit, pulsing with anticipation. Just before the clock struck twelve, a familiar voice rang out near the front.

"Christ is Risen."

It was Father Andreas Pappas. Calm. Quiet. Unmistakable.

He lit his candle.

Then one by one, the flames spread. Through the pews, out to the aisles, around the narthex, and into the courtyard. Even the smallest children stood reverent. Paul lit his candle from Helena's. The boys lit theirs from Paul.

They carried the flame home carefully. Helena placed it in a tall glass by the icon stand. "Keep it burning," she said, tucking the boys into bed. "That's the whole point."

The year that followed was a quiet one. Helena grew thinner. Slower. The music stayed on in the house, and so did the laughter, but something in the air shifted. She didn't talk about what was happening, and neither did Paul. They didn't name it. They didn't need to.

She passed peacefully before the leaves turned gold, her hand in Paul's, the boys close by. There was no hospital bed. No dramatic goodbye. Just her home, her candle, and a quiet knowing. She was buried in the Greek section at Keilor East cemetery, beneath the olive tree she had always loved.

What she had told the Avery men before she left stayed with them. She had kissed the boys' foreheads and said, "You live on. You live fully. I will always be here."

The next Easter, Paul and the boys stood outside the church in silence.

They didn't speak. They didn't need to.

At midnight, Father Pappa again stepped forward.

"Christ is Risen."

A single flame. Then two. Then hundreds.

Paul's candle was lit by someone he didn't see. His hands trembled. Tears came. The boys turned to him, voices low.

"Mum is here."

"She'll always be."

They embraced. Candles in hand. Hearts in pieces and yet somehow still whole.

And the light spread again, not just through the churchyard, but through memory.

Through love.

Through Helena.

A light that did not go out.

Justice Brady – Jury Instructions – Not Perfect, Just Human

The courtroom smelled faintly of old timber and colder mornings. Light from the skylights slanted across the jury box, striping the jurors' folded hands and solemn faces.

At the bench, Justice Kimberly Brady adjusted her robe with a careful, precise tug. Her expression was composed, her posture straight but not stiff. She glanced once at the accused – a slight woman with dark eyes and bruised arms hidden under the sleeves of a borrowed blouse – and then turned back to the jury.

Twelve pairs of eyes lifted to meet hers. Some weary, some just tired, but all waiting.

Kimberly's voice, when it came, was steady and unforced.

"You have heard all the evidence. It is now time for me to direct you on the law you must apply. Nothing I say about the facts is binding on you. But on the law – you must accept and apply it, as I explain."

She paused, letting the courtroom settle around her words.

"The burden rests entirely on the prosecution. It is for them to prove, beyond a reasonable doubt, that the accused committed the offence charged. The accused has nothing to prove."

She let her eyes move briefly across the bar table, where the prosecutor was rearranging his notes with a restless thumb, and where the defence counsel sat, hands clasped in silent readiness.

"You are considering a charge of intentionally causing serious injury," she continued, her tone even, her delivery deliberate. "For the prosecution to succeed, they must prove beyond reasonable doubt that the accused caused serious injury to the victim, and that she did so with intent."

She drew a breath – not from fatigue, but from carefulness.

"But this case turns, most of all, on **self-defence**."

There was a shift among the jurors. A lean forward. A breath caught. A pencil paused over a notepad.

"Since 2005," Kimberly said, "our law has changed to better recognise the realities of family violence. You are entitled – indeed, you are required – to consider those realities when deciding whether the accused acted in lawful self-defence."

The accused, sitting silently in the dock, barely moved. Only the faint tightening of her fingers around the edge of the table betrayed her attention.

"You must ask yourselves two questions," Kimberly said.

"First: Did the accused believe that her actions were necessary to defend herself from harm?"

She glanced at the jury – not challenging them, but inviting them to consider it carefully.

"Her belief does not have to be correct. It does not have to be wise. It only needs to be genuine. Formed honestly, in the moment, based on her experience – and what she knew of the man standing over her."

A brief, deliberate pause.

"Second: Was her belief – when judged in the full context of her life and the violence she had endured – a reasonable one?"

She stepped out from behind the bench, moving to the front of the court in her black robes, not reading now, but speaking directly, as if each juror was seated across a kitchen table, trusted with something sacred.

"You have heard evidence of their relationship," she said softly.

"Of past violence. Of threats. Of the fear that does not begin and end with one night but bleeds into every morning."

"You must not think: *Why didn't she leave?* You must not think: *Why didn't she run?* You must ask: **Given her world, her history, her fear – was it reasonable for her to believe she had no choice?**"

A woman in the second row of the jury dabbed at her eye with a tissue.

Kimberly did not pause.

"In cases involving family violence, the law recognises that danger does not always come announced. That fear can sit in the walls. That survival does not always look clean, or perfect, or rehearsed."

She stepped back behind the bench, smoothing the front of her robes with a single small gesture.

Her next words were measured – but not cold.

"If you are satisfied that the accused believed her actions were necessary, and that belief was reasonable in all the circumstances, then she acted lawfully. You must find her **not guilty**."

"If you hold a reasonable doubt on either question – you must find her **not guilty**."

"Only if you are sure, beyond reasonable doubt, that she neither genuinely believed nor reasonably believed it was necessary to act – only then may you find her **guilty**."

She let the silence grow heavy and whole before she added, more quietly: "Law is not blind to imperfection. Justice does not demand that a frightened woman calculate threat with precision, or that she act as a philosopher might."

Her gaze was steady.

“Law demands only that we understand what it is to be human.”

A moment later, she nodded to the foreperson.

“You may now retire to consider your verdict.”

The clerk rose. The bailiff opened the jury room door.

As the twelve filed out, Kimberly sat back, hands folded lightly before her.

She watched them go – twelve ordinary people carrying an extraordinary weight.

And in the dock, the accused exhaled, a slow shudder of breath – the first in hours.

Outside, the bells of St Patrick’s Cathedral tolled noon.

Inside, the County Court waited to see what justice would look like when it wore no mask.

Brady Family – California Adventure

Kimberly barely remembered dropping the raffle ticket into the box – she had been late for a case meeting, her hair half-dried, scribbling 'K Brady' on the stub while telling Sarah to run inside. The fundraiser was for the new science wing at Mentone Girls, and buying a ticket had seemed the right thing to do.

A month later, the call came.

"You've won first prize," a voice from the Parents' Committee announced, tinged with delighted disbelief. "A family holiday to California!"

Kimberly stood frozen in her chambers, the phone in one hand, a pen poised above case files. "Is this a joke?"

"No, Ms Brady. It's real."

And just like that, something inside her shifted. For the first time in months, Kimberly laughed – a real laugh, the kind Sarah would later describe: "Mum, you sounded like your old self."

The trip was booked. It was hers. It was theirs.

Three months later, holding her youngest's hand through the Arrivals gate at LAX, Kimberly shed her judicial robes for a different identity: mother, traveller, dreamer. Carry-on packed with sunscreen, cereal bars, and hope, she stepped into America.

For once, she didn't have to plan every moment. She only had to follow the adventure.

That night, Kimberly sat in the hotel room with a notepad, just as her father used to when he finished counting fruit crates and checking ledgers. She drew a heavy line across the page – a habit she'd inherited without knowing.

Above the line: destinations, times, entry fees, weather forecasts, and estimated fuel. Every box, dutifully ticked.

Below the line: space. Empty. Open.

Carefully, she wrote two words:

What if?

Sarah, already curled on her side, watched koi fish videos on her laptop, oblivious.

Kimberly sat still.

The pen lay idle, but her thoughts surged.

What if we have more days like this?

What if I can be both a judge and a joyful mum?

What if this is just the beginning?

What if I'm allowed to be happy again – not someday, but now?

She didn't need to write it all. The two words were enough.

What if?

The Rock

They called it a prison.

But Kimberly understood it had always been a fortress.

She stepped off the ferry, Nick's small hand clutching hers. The Bay air was sharp, salt-laced, clean – and heavy with old pain. The Rock rose from the water: stone, silence, memory.

Built to keep enemies out. Later, to trap men within.

She wasn't sure which was sadder.

Inside, the audio tour droned through their headphones. Sarah and Josh drifted ahead, but Kimberly moved slowly, deliberately. She wanted to feel it – the stone underfoot, the iron bars, the chill seeping through broken windows.

"This cell once belonged to inmate #AZ1476," the recording said. "He spent twenty-two years here. On New Year's Eve, prisoners said they could hear laughter and music from San Francisco – a world they could see but never touch."

Kimberly paused at that cell. Rust rimmed the stainless steel sink. A narrow cot stood against the wall.

So close to life. And utterly walled away from it.

Just like she had been, once.

Handing down sentences in courtrooms while her own heart remained locked away. Watching her children's lives through the glass pane of responsibility. Seeing freedom – weekends, spontaneity, softness – but never reaching for it.

Because she had built a fortress around herself.

"Mum?"

Sarah's voice, gentle, tugged at her.

"You okay?"

Kimberly blinked and nodded. "Just thinking."

"About the prisoners?"

"About the walls we build," she whispered.

They stepped into the prison yard. Across the glittering bay, the city thrummed with life: cable cars rattling, lovers strolling, music drifting over Golden Gate Park.

Freedom – a twenty-minute ferry away.

Yet for those trapped here, utterly unreachable.

"It's not just a jail," Kimberly murmured. "It's a fortress."

Sarah studied her.

"Are you talking about this place… or about you?"

Kimberly didn't answer.

She didn't need to.

The tour continued deeper into the heart of Alcatraz – corridors lined with narrow cells, stacked like forgotten drawers in a filing cabinet of punishment.

Kimberly kept Nick tucked close. Sarah wandered slightly behind, her phone idle in her hand.

Josh stopped.

He stood staring into a small, windowless cell, a bed barely wide enough to stretch out on.

"Mum," he said quietly.

Kimberly slipped off her headset. "Yes, love?"

Josh pointed into the empty cell.

"Is this where you send the bad people?"

The words, so soft and unsure, struck harder than any steel bar.

Kimberly crouched beside him.

"Josh…" she said gently.

"You're a judge. You send people to jail."

He wasn't accusing. He was trying to understand.

She nodded slowly. "Yes, I do."

Josh looked up at her, his eyes dark with confusion.

Kimberly followed his gaze into the cold, narrow space: the cot, the sink, the walls that kept someone locked away.

She reached for the right words.

"The places I send them aren't like this," she said carefully. "They have real rooms. Some have TVs. They can work, learn a trade, study, even speak to their families – sometimes see their kids."

"They're not there to be forgotten."

Josh was quiet, thinking hard.

"So jail's not about hurting them?" he asked.

"No," Kimberly said softly. "It's about stopping harm. Protecting others. Giving someone a chance to come back better than when they went in."

Josh's little face tightened in thought.

"But… do you still care about them?"

Kimberly smiled sadly.

She touched his cheek, brushing her fingers along his skin.

"I do, Josh. I don't stop seeing the human being. I look them in the eye. I listen to them. I remember they once had a mother, just like you do."

Josh leaned into her side, quiet for a moment.

Then he asked, almost in a whisper:

"Do you ever cry when you do it?"

Kimberly's throat tightened. She swallowed hard.

"Sometimes," she whispered. "Afterwards."

Josh pressed closer to her, his small hand finding hers.

And for the first time in a long while, Kimberly Brady didn't feel like a fortress of stone and duty.

She simply felt human – soft, breakable, and still capable of hope.

That night, back at their San Francisco hotel, Kimberly opened her notebook.

Under a neat checklist:

- Clam chowder
- Cable cars
- The Rock

She drew a line.

Beneath it, she wrote:

What if… I could leave the fortress, too?

Wharves, Wishes, and Wonder

The fog had begun to lift by noon, revealing the golden shoulders of the city beneath it. Cable car bells rang through the air like dinner chimes, and Kimberly bought four one-way tickets at the Powell Street turnaround while the kids watched the operator spin the whole car on a wooden turntable.

"That's so old-fashioned," Sarah said, raising her phone to take a video.

"It's called heritage," Kimberly replied with a small smile.

Nick squealed as they climbed aboard and gripped the brass rail. "We're really standing! We're really standing, Mum!"

"Just hang on!" Kimberly laughed. "And don't let go if we go downhill fast."

Josh looked unimpressed. "This thing's like a train that forgot what it was doing."

"It's charming," Kimberly said, brushing his hair back. "Let it charm you."

"I'll try," Josh muttered, gripping the pole with one hand and keeping the other firmly tucked into his jacket pocket.

Fisherman's Wharf: Clam Chowder and Civilisation

After the hills, laughter, and windblown hair, they landed near Fisherman's Wharf. A row of food stalls greeted them, all advertising the same thing: Clam Chowder in a Sourdough Bowl – Boudin's Famous!

"Okay, everybody choose your lunch," Kimberly said.

Sarah immediately got in line for chowder. Nick followed, tugging at Kimberly's arm.

"I want the bread bowl! I want to eat the bowl!"

Kimberly smiled. "That's the spirit."

Josh stared at the menu, wrinkling his nose at the steaming white soup being ladled into hollowed-out loaves.

"Mum," he said flatly, "that smells like the ocean's old socks."

Kimberly laughed out loud. "It's seafood chowder, darling. It's delicious."

"It's fish milk," Josh declared. "I want a hot dog."

"You're in San Francisco, and you're choosing a hot dog?" Kimberly teased.

"It's a safe food, Mum."

Kimberly threw up her hands. "All right, one hot dog coming up for our resident food critic."

Minutes later, they sat on a bench overlooking the bay. Seagulls screeched in the sky above, and a street saxophonist played 'When the Saints Go Marching In'.

Sarah dipped her bread bowl with a thoughtful look. Nick had chowder on his nose. Josh unwrapped his foil and took a triumphant bite.

"This," he announced, "is civilisation."

Kimberly shook her head. "You're lucky you're charming."

"So's the hotdog," Josh said, and Sarah captured the moment with a photo – brothers on either side, the sea sparkling behind them.

Los Angeles Dreams

The road stretched long and golden as they drove south along Highway 101, leaving behind the fog-wrapped hills of San Francisco. Palm trees lined the streets like sentinels, and every mile felt warmer, looser, freer.

"Mum, are we going to see movie stars?" Nick asked from the back seat, his new Minion cap slightly askew.

"If we do, act cool," Kimberly said, smiling in the rearview mirror.

"Define cool," Josh said dryly.

"No pointing," Sarah added. "And no shouting."

Nick nodded solemnly. "I'll just wave."

Kimberly laughed, the sound feeling easier than it had days ago.

Universal Studios: Robots, Wizards, and Presidents

The sun was high when they stepped onto the main boulevard of Universal Studios. Music blared, signs flashed, and crowds bustled with excitement – popcorn buckets, butterbeer mugs, foam wands in every direction.

"Where first?" Kimberly asked.

"Harry Potter!" Sarah said immediately, then glanced around. "I mean… if that's okay."

"Very okay." Kimberly smiled.

They hurried toward the Wizarding World of Harry Potter, passing beneath towering gates and cobblestone streets. Nick's eyes widened as he gripped his chocolate frog like it might fly away.

After spells, wands, and a ride through Hogwarts, Josh tugged Kimberly toward the Transformers attraction.

"It's 3D and fast and has robots that talk," he said breathlessly. "Like, actual robots. One of them might even be the President."

Kimberly raised an eyebrow. "That sounds terrifying."

"It's amazing," Josh insisted.

Inside the dark ride queue, he narrated the backstory with the passion of a true believer.

"Mum," he whispered as they boarded. "You have to save the AllSpark. Just believe in Optimus Prime, okay?"

"I believe in you," she whispered back.

The ride was chaos – sharp turns, explosions of light, shouted orders – and Josh gripped the safety bar, grinning from ear to ear.

"Mr President!" he shouted at an animatronic general. "Do something!"

Afterwards, they stumbled off the ride, breathless.

"Best thing ever," Josh declared. "Robots. Presidents. And Mum screamed again."

"I didn't scream," Kimberly said, smoothing her hair.

"You did a legal objection yell," Sarah teased.

Kimberly smiled, flushed. "Sustained."

Kung Fu Panda and Popcorn

Later, they shared a giant popcorn bucket during the *Kung Fu Panda* show. The theatre darkened, and animated lanterns floated around them in glowing patterns.

Sarah leaned against Kimberly's shoulder.

"You're laughing," she said.

"I know," Kimberly replied.

"You never laugh that loud at home."

Kimberly paused, feeling the truth of it.

"Maybe I should," she said softly.

Sarah didn't reply, but she smiled and nestled closer.

Memory Lane: Spielberg's Red Coat

While waiting for the studio tram tour, Kimberly's gaze caught a simple, haunting image on a mural – a little girl in a red coat.

She stared, her heart tightening.

Sarah noticed.

"I saw that in history class," Sarah said quietly.

"You watched the whole film?" Kimberly asked.

"Only part. But I remember her."

Kimberly nodded. "So do I."

The queue shuffled forward, but for a moment, Kimberly stayed still.

In a place built on fantasy and rides, this piece of history remained – and she was grateful.

Because joy doesn't mean forgetting.

And storytelling can be sacred.

She looked again at the little girl in red.

"He used colour to remind us she mattered," Kimberly whispered.

Sarah squeezed her hand.

"And now we don't forget."

The tram pulled up, and the ride began – but Kimberly tucked the image into her heart, where no camera could reach.

Disneyland Days

Day One: Main Street and Wonder

The moment they stepped through the gates, Nicholas stopped walking.

"Mum…" he whispered, "is this the real one?"

"The only one, sweetheart."

Main Street smelled like popcorn and sugar, the buildings trimmed with bunting and painted hope. A marching band came around the corner, red coats gleaming, brass instruments catching the sun.

Sarah stopped in her tracks.

"They're singing."

"Barbershop quartet," Kimberly said. "Old-fashioned."

"It's beautiful."

For a long second, Sarah didn't take a photo. She just watched.

"Are you crying?" Josh whispered to her.

"Shut up," she replied, wiping her cheek.

Day Two: Rides, Rain, and Dancing in the Street

It rained just enough to make the footpaths glisten. Kimberly bought ponchos. Nick wore his backwards.

They rode Space Mountain and Buzz Lightyear, stood in line for over an hour just to meet Mickey, and ate too many churros.

In the afternoon, a sudden burst of sun hit the puddles on Main Street. The parade started – not scheduled, not announced. Just… there.

And Sarah – Sarah who hated dancing in PE, who but always auditioned for school musicals – stepped forward when the music swelled.

"Sarah over the sings dans," Nicholas said proudly, pointing.

"That's Sarah dancing to the singing," Kimberly translated, heart swelling.

And she was. Sarah danced. Nothing dramatic – just a sway, a smile, a hand raised to ward the music.

"You look beautiful," Kimberly whispered.

Sarah laughed and spun once on the wet pavement.

"It's Main Street," she said. "I have to."

Day Three: Wishes, Fireworks, and Farewell

The last night came too quickly.

They watched the fireworks from in front of the castle – Nick on Kimberly's hip again, even though he was heavy now. Josh had bought light-up Mickey ears. Sarah filmed the first five seconds, then lowered her phone and just watched.

"Make a wish," Kimberly said quietly.

"I don't need to," Sarah replied. "I think it's already happening."

Kimberly blinked away the sting behind her eyes.

It really had taken three days.

One to get there.

One to believe it was real.

And one to remember forever.

The Huntington Library

The Power of the Printed Word

It was just the two of them.

Kimberly had arranged for Nicholas and Josh to stay at the hotel's childcare program – a half-day adventure with crafts, cartoons, and pizza.

"You sure you don't mind?" she'd asked Sarah that morning.

"Spending a whole day with just me?"

Sarah shrugged, but there was a softness behind it. "I want to."

They drove the rental car along tree-lined streets until the signs for The Huntington Library appeared – tucked into manicured grounds and spring-blooming roses.

The Hall of Treasures

Inside the Library Exhibition Hall, the air was cool and reverent. Voices lowered themselves without being asked.

"Over here," Kimberly said quietly, gesturing toward a glass case at the centre of the room.

Sarah followed.

There it was.

The Gutenberg Bible.

Open. Preserved. Glowing softly under golden light.

Sarah leaned in, scanning the Latin text, the hand-painted initials, the thick paper that had survived six centuries.

"It looks like it was made yesterday," she said.

"It changed the world," Kimberly whispered. "Before this, books were copied by hand. This… this was the first time knowledge could spread faster than one person could write."

Sarah didn't speak. But she stood there for a long time.

Kimberly's Inner Voice

Kimberly stared through the glass, remembering courtrooms and closing statements, notebooks and bedtime stories.

We don't realise how powerful it is, she thought, to write something down. To preserve it. To pass it on.

The Gutenberg wasn't large or flashy.

But it had survived.

Because someone believed words mattered.

And here she was, standing beside her daughter – a girl who might one day use her own voice to shape the world.

A Quiet Exchange

"Mum," Sarah said, still staring at the page, "do you ever worry your words won't be remembered?"

Kimberly looked at her – really looked at her.

"Every day," she said.

Sarah nodded. "Me too."

Kimberly smiled, but it was quiet and full of truth.

"But they don't need to be famous to matter. They just need to be true."

(A Starlight Surprise!)

This was meant to be a quiet night.

As they wandered through Downtown LA after dinner – no plans, no pressure.

"Can we just walk?" Sarah had asked.

"I like walking," Nicholas said. "It's like slow running."

They laughed and strolled along, past neon signs and bustling sidewalks, until they passed a theatre tucked between taller, shinier buildings.

A small sign in the glass:

TONIGHT ONLY – RUSH TICKETS – STARLIGHT EXPRESS

Kimberly stopped in her tracks.

"I haven't seen that since university," she murmured.

"What is it?" Josh asked.

"It's a musical. With trains. And roller skates."

"REAL roller skates?" Nicholas asked, wide-eyed.

"Real everything," Kimberly smiled.

She looked at the kids. Looked at the sign.

Looked down at her notebook, still tucked in her bag.

Then said:

"What if… we just go in?"

And they did.

Inside the Theatre: Magic for All Ages

The lights dimmed. The music swelled.

Joshua's mouth fell open the moment the first train rolled on stage – actors in shimmering costumes, racing and singing at the same time.

"Mum, they're skating and singing!" he whispered loudly.

"It's like watching race cars with music!" Nick added, bouncing in his seat.

Sarah tried to look unimpressed.

She failed by Act Two.

"Okay," she whispered during intermission. "This is kind of amazing."

Kimberly laughed. "Kind of?"

"The music is cheesy," Sarah insisted.

"It's Andrew Lloyd Webber. It's allowed."

"Still."

But Sarah couldn't stop smiling.

Neither could Kimberly.

Not during the finale, when the stage filled with colour and speed and shining faces.

Not afterwards, when Nicholas tried skating in his sneakers all the way back to the hotel.

And not later that night, when Kimberly opened her notebook again – drawing one last heavy line across the page.

Above the line: every place they'd been. Every ticket stub, every photograph, every laugh.

Below the line: blank, beautiful space.

And three simple words:

What if… always?

Justice Brady – The Robe and the Gavel

Her chambers were quiet – not silent, never that – but composed in the rhythm of her work. Legal briefs lay in neat piles, a red pencil rested diagonally across an open judgment draft, and the scent of Earl Grey hung faintly in the air, forgotten in its cup beside a half-read case authority.

The city murmured beyond the tall windows, but inside these sandstone walls, time moved differently – slow, deliberate, heavy with responsibility.

Kimberly sat poised at her desk, her concentration undisturbed, until a soft buzz cut through the quiet.

"Your Honour," came Henry's voice, crisp through the intercom. "The Chief Justice is on the line for you."

Her hand stilled over the page. The pencil was placed down gently.

"Thank you, Henry. Please put her through."

There was a *click*, and then a second of silence before the Chief Justice's voice filled the receiver – steady, formal, unmistakable.

"Justice Brady, I am calling on behalf of the Governor of Victoria. It is my duty and privilege to inform you that, acting on the recommendation of the Attorney-General and with the approval of the Executive Council, Her Excellency the Governor has appointed you as a judge of the Supreme Court of Victoria.

"Your appointment takes effect immediately, and arrangements will be made for your formal swearing-in at the Court next week.

"On behalf of the judiciary, I extend my sincere congratulations. Your elevation is well-deserved, and the Court will be strengthened by your presence on the bench."

Kimberly stood as the words settled over her like a robe being placed upon her shoulders. She held the receiver in both hands – not out of nervousness, but reverence.

"Thank you, Chief Justice," she replied quietly. "It is an honour beyond measure. I will serve the Court with all that I am – faithfully, and to the best of my judgment."

"I have every confidence you will," came the reply. "We look forward to welcoming you formally. Good morning, Justice Brady."

Click.

The line fell silent.

Her chambers, so familiar and workmanlike, now felt transformed. Kimberly's eyes moved to the window, where the morning light crept through, soft and golden.

Outside, the city carried on – trams humming, footsteps on pavement, coats drawn tight against the winter chill. No fanfare. No headlines. But inside this room, everything had changed.

She touched the top of her desk with her fingertips – steady, grounding.

This was no triumph. It was a trust.

The pen would feel heavier now. Each judgment, each sentence, each silence from the bench would matter more than ever. And yet, in the quiet of that moment, she did not feel burdened. She felt ready.

Somewhere beyond the Court, Sarah would still be in class. She would tell her that night – not with speeches or ceremony, but in their small kitchen over dinner. Maybe Sarah would look at her differently. Maybe not. Kimberly hoped it would be the latter.

She looked down at the files on her desk and whispered, almost to herself: “Let’s begin.”

One Week Later – The Banco Court

The corridors of the Supreme Court held their breath that morning.

Clerks moved like shadows in pressed suits. Robes were dusted, ties straightened, wigs set just so. In the grand Banco Court, where the portraits of justices past lined the timber-panelled walls, the room was already full before the hour struck.

Every pew was filled – barristers in silk and junior counsel in dark suits, judges robed and seated in solemn anticipation, and a handful of reporters whose pens already hovered over notepads. The air smelled faintly of old wood, starched linen, and history.

Then came the gentle rustle of movement as the side door opened. A hush swept over the room.

Justice Kimberly Judith Brady entered – flanked by two court officers, robe trailing, expression composed but not cold. Her chin lifted slightly as she took in the sea of faces: friends, colleagues, adversaries turned well-wishers.

In the front row sat her parents, hands folded, eyes shining. Her mother wore a deep navy dress, hat pinned neatly, her pearls understated but proud. Her father looked like a man restraining himself from standing to applaud. Beside them sat Sarah, her school uniform replaced with a simple blue dress and ballet flats. She swung her legs slowly – not in boredom, but in quiet excitement.

And then there was James.

He stood as she entered, as tradition demanded. His suit was impeccable, his expression unreadable – a trained lawyer's mask. But Kimberly noticed it: the subtle tightening of his jaw, the faint sigh as he sat back down. He was here because he knew what this moment demanded – from the father of her children, from the son of a legal dynasty, from the man whose name she still carried, though their marriage had long since dissolved in silence and fatigue.

The ceremony began.

The Associate read the commission aloud, every word echoing through the court with the clarity of finality:

"Her Excellency, the Honourable Linda Dessau, Governor of Victoria, acting on the advice of the Executive Council, has appointed Kimberly Judith Brady as a Judge of the Supreme Court of Victoria…"

Each clause landed like a bell toll – solemn, beautiful, binding.

The Chief Justice spoke next, her voice strong, clear, and proud:

"Justice Brady comes to this Court after distinguished service in the County Court and a career marked by diligence, compassion, and intellectual strength. Her Honour's rulings have consistently reflected a deep understanding of the law and its impact on people's lives."

Kimberly listened – not for the praise, but for the responsibility embedded within it.

Then it was her turn.

She stood, eyes scanning no one in particular and everyone at once.

"Chief Justice, fellow justices, members of the Bar, distinguished guests – I thank you for this honour. Today, I stand here not as the culmination of one journey, but as the custodian of a continuing one.

"Justice is not a title; it is a burden we choose. And I will bear it with all the integrity I can offer. I thank my mentors, who taught me that restraint is as important as reason. I thank my parents, whose faith has never faltered.

"And to my daughter, Sarah – your questions have shaped my answers. I hope one day you will find your own.

"To those with whom I have shared years – friends, colleagues, even those with whom I have debated across the aisle – thank you. You have sharpened me."

There was a pause. Just a beat. And then:

"And to James – thank you for being here. For our shared past and for Sarah's future."

James inclined his head slightly, acknowledging the weight and grace of her words. It was not forgiveness, and it was not a truce. But it was peace, of a kind.

The court rose in unison – the long tradition of welcoming a new judge with the warmth of a standing ovation in silence. No clapping. Just presence.

In that moment, as the robe settled around her and her gaze swept across the courtroom, Kimberly felt not triumphant – but still.

This was not a victory.

It was a vow.

Sarah Brady – Mentone Girls Grammar

It was the final term of Year 12 at Mentone Girls' Grammar. Sarah had grown up in Brighton until the age of ten, a childhood spent among manicured lawns, seaside breezes, and elegant uniforms from Prep to Year 12. She had attended Mentone Girls' Grammar – one of Melbourne's elite independent schools, known for its tradition, strength, and quiet ambition, as well as its significant fees. After the divorce, Sarah's father agreed to subsidise the school fees. Even with Kimberly's judicial salary, the cost of such an education would have been a major burden alone – but both parents had agreed early on that Sarah's schooling should continue without disruption. Like most top-tier private schools, it boasted a strong academic reputation and a highly competitive sports program. Sarah had struggled at times with the relentless demands of after-school sport – swimming, athletics, netball, all part of the culture – but she never complained. She stayed strong, quietly determined. What she truly loved, however, were the academic and arts programs.

She was in every school production from Year 7 onwards, and in Year 12, she took on the lead role in the final school play – a performance that drew praise from both teachers and peers. Her mother was always there in the front row, and so was Kimberly's mother – Sarah's Nana – who became the unofficial wardrobe mistress. When the Year 9 production of *Peter Pan* needed a crocodile costume on short notice, Nana delivered it overnight, asking only, 'How big should the teeth be?' She sewed like a professional and treated each play like a West End debut. Great Nana had passed away when Sarah was very young, so Nana – Kimberly's mum – became a central figure in their lives. After the divorce, she was more than a wardrobe mistress – she helped Kimberly raise three children while Kimberly returned to full-time work. She managed school pick-ups, made costumes late into the night, and filled their Oakleigh home with practical care and quiet devotion.

That was where she came alive, where her mind found room to explore, where she felt closest to her mother's world. A school known for its tradition, strength, and quiet ambition... But after her parents' divorce, her mother – Kimberly – bought a modest weatherboard house in Oakleigh. Kimberly, ever the strategist, had planned it carefully – the location was no accident. It was the kind of decision that showed not just practicality but foresight – the hallmark of a smart woman who always thought three moves ahead. The house sat a short walk from Warrigal Road, giving Sarah a straightforward bus ride to Mentone Girls' Grammar each morning. Kimberly knew even then that continuity mattered. Sarah moved there with her younger brother Joshua and baby Nicholas, the rhythms of family life changing, but never losing their warmth or strength.

Sarah Brady stood just beneath the Wall of Honour in the school foyer, straightening her uniform blazer with a practised tug. Above her, Sarah imagined a new addition to the Wall of Honour – a painting that did not yet exist, and never would, at least not on these walls. Kimberly had never attended Mentone Girls' Grammar, so she would not be honoured here formally. But in Sarah's mind, the image appeared vividly: her mother, The Honourable Justice Kimberly Judith Brady, in full judicial gown and wig, seated with quiet dignity, a beautiful smile softening her eyes. A gold plaque beneath read: 'The Honourable Justice Kimberly Judith Brady – Supreme Court of Victoria.'

The Wall of Honour was nestled just outside the school's beautiful auditorium, where art exhibitions and school plays were held, and where every graduate had once spoken their farewell words. It featured portraits of Mentone Girls' most distinguished alumnae: authors, surgeons, judges and even a former Premier of Victoria. Sarah had walked past them all – hundreds of times over her school years. Sometimes in a rush, sometimes deep in thought. But one quiet day not long ago, when the hallway had been empty and her blazer still smelled faintly of lavender from Nana's wash, she had stopped and looked up. For the first time, she allowed herself to wonder – could she see herself up there, twenty years from now? Would they see her? Her flashy father, James Brady, who once declared on national television that 'at James Brady & Associates fight for justice' – always in the most expensive fitted suit money could buy. Or her mother, sitting quietly on the Supreme Court bench, robes still impeccable, gaze unwavering. Not as Kimberly's daughter. Not as a shadow. But as Sarah Elizabeth Brady – in her own frame, in her own right.

The school was buzzing with preparation for the Graduation Assembly. Blazers had been brushed. Ribbons and pins polished. Sarah had been chosen to deliver the opening reading – a piece about legacy and service, written by a former Head Prefect.

She knew why they'd chosen her.

Not just because of the grades. Not just because she was Kimberly Brady's daughter. But because – like her mother – she was calm, clear, and quietly certain.

In the crowd of bustling Year 12s adjusting speeches and smoothing skirts, Sarah stood out for being still. Her friends joked that she had 'bench energy' – poised, collected, a natural listener.

Teachers trusted her without needing reminders. Younger students watched her the way junior associates watched a lead counsel – not afraid, just quietly impressed.

Her mother would be seated in the front row that afternoon. Not as a guest of honour. Not as the judge. Just as a mother – holding a program, smiling softly, and likely holding back tears.

At lunch, Sarah sat under the jacaranda tree near the science wing, tapping her pen against a page of notes. She wasn't rehearsing the speech – she knew it cold. Instead, she was jotting down a few thoughts for her personal reflection project: a letter to her younger self.

"You will be known first as your mother's daughter," she wrote. "But that won't be a weight. It will be a compass."

"And one day, someone will call you Judge Brady – not because you followed her path, but because you found your own through hers."

She smiled.

Melbourne Uni Law – Not Perfect, Just Learning

Note:
A classroom is not a forum for adjudication. It is a forum for analysis.

If the full rules of evidence applied, students could only repeat what the jury heard, and the exercise would be limited to description rather than understanding. The purpose of this chapter is to examine strategy, silence, and consequence – all of which require looking beyond the transcript.

Melbourne Law Tutorial Room – Mid-Morning

The room smelled like eucalyptus hand sanitiser and burnt espresso – the modern perfume of law school mornings. Twenty students were scattered around two long tables pushed into a hollow square, half already clicking open MacBooks, others flipping through marked-up court transcripts, printed double-sided and stapled like undergrad battle plans.

The windows looked out over University Square, but the blinds were mostly down. The light was too stark for comfort.

A group of five clustered on the far side – all cuffed blazers and whispered in-jokes, their highlighters in matching pastel shades. One had already bookmarked the DPP website. Another, earbuds still half-in, was Googling *Kimberly Brady* on her phone.

At the opposite end, a student in a hoodie was bent over a transcript, notes crammed into the margins:

s 322K – reasonable belief? vs actual threat?

A few hovered in between – watching, listening. Not quite in any group, but too smart to show it mattered.

The professor entered five minutes late, balancing a long black and a stack of well-thumbed notes. She didn't speak right away. Just scanned the room – the glowing screens, the paper cuts, the defensive body language – and smiled faintly, like someone watching actors forget they're being watched.

"So," she said finally, setting her coffee down. "*R v Jarra.* A trial about knives, fear, and what happens when imperfection walks into a courtroom."

Someone snorted. A cough covered it. The professor continued, unfazed.

"I asked you to read the transcripts. I didn't ask you to decide guilt. I asked you to sit in that room – with Ms Brady, with the accused, with the Crown – and ask yourselves what it meant."

Zara frowned as she flipped through her transcript. "The defence is run by… K Brady," she said, pointing at the line.

Then her eyes widened slightly. She stared at the page, and then up again.

"Wait. Is this… *Justice* Kimberly Brady's case?"

A few students turned, surprised. One scrolled quickly on their phone. Confirmed.

The professor didn't smile. She just met Zara's gaze, evenly.

"At the time," she said, "she was just a Legal Aid solicitor."

She tapped her pencil once, gently.

"Now? Now it's Justice Brady's case. Because she didn't make it about herself – but every decision she made still echoes through how we teach it today."

Zara blinked, then gave a small, triumphant fist bump to herself. "Oh, go girl," she murmured, a grin spreading across her face.

From John in the back, "Wait – wasn't she a commercial litigator?"

The professor replies:

"Yes. A very good one. But this case – Jarra – this is why she's in the curriculum. Not because she made money. Because she made a difference."

A girl in tortoiseshell glasses leaned back, arms crossed.

"I mean, she stabbed him eight times."

Across from her, the hoodie student murmured:

"And sat down afterwards. Didn't run."

"Because she was high," someone else muttered.

The professor raised an eyebrow.

"Because she was scared," she said. "But we'll get there."

Character evidence not led. Remand incident excluded. Strategy or necessity?

The professor smirked slightly.

"Good. Because today's not about legal correctness. It's about discomfort. And how much of it the system allows – or ignores."

She walked to the side of the whiteboard and wrote four words:

FEAR. FORCE. JUDGMENT. TRUTH.

"Jarra. Her Honour. And everyone in that courtroom had to choose what those words meant. You'll have to, too."

She looked up again – this time more pointedly.

"So, who wants to go first?"

Silence. A chair creaked.

Then Zara raised her hand.

Picking Apart the Transcript – and What's Missing

The rustle of paper echoed softly under the hum of laptops. Highlighters paused. Screens scrolled.

Zara flipped back through her copy, fingers quick, brows drawn.

"Has anyone found it yet? The character references?"

Priya looked up. "What do you mean?"

"Good character. There's no reference to it – not in Her Honour's openings, not in the cross-examinations, not even in the jury directions. No past employer. No rehab sponsor. No neighbour. Nothing."

Dan tapped the edge of his printout.

"Page 123. There's a mention of someone named Mrs Salas. A possible character witness. But she never appears."

The professor interjected from the front.

"Correct. The defence flagged a character list – then didn't call a single one."

Silence.

Zara frowned. "But why? That's textbook defensive scaffolding. Humanise the client. Soften the jury."

Professor: "This is not in the transcript, but I know that an incident happened in remand. Jarra broke another remand prisoner's fingers in a fight in the yard."

Dan nodded. "Especially when you're up against eight stab wounds."

Lian: "If Justice Brady had put Jarra's character in issue, the Crown could've brought in the prison incident. The broken finger. That rage."

Priya shook her head. "But still – there had to be someone who could speak to who she was before."

The professor finally responded. "There was. But character evidence isn't a free swing. Once you open that door, you can't control who walks through it."

She let that sit, then added:

"Her Honour made a choice. She didn't argue that her client was good. She argued her client was afraid."

Zara glanced down, flipping pages again. "It's all right here. Page 212. Closing address: *'Not because she's perfect. But because the law allows for imperfection when the truth is complicated, and the fear is real.'*"

Dan murmured: "That's the line."

Liam leaned back, voice low. "Justice Brady defended a woman the jury couldn't admire. Only understand."

The class had grown quieter, more focused. Notes were being refined. Highlighters capped. Screens flicked between legislation tabs and court indexes. A kind of reverent concentration had settled – until Zara leaned back, frowning.

"Professor… there's a gap."

The professor looked up from her own printout. "Go on."

Zara held up her bundle of stapled pages. "We've got cross-exams, closing addresses, even sidebar arguments noted in chambers. But no mention of the remand incident. Not one line about the broken finger."

A few heads turned. Dan blinked. "Wait – you're saying that fight wasn't part of the evidence?"

A few students turned to their laptops. Clicking started. One whispered: "That changes everything."

The professor didn't move. Just watched them work through it.

"Changes it?" she repeated evenly. "How?"

John jumped in. “Well, it damages her credibility, obviously. Makes her seem volatile. If that had come out at trial–”

“She might’ve lost,” Priya said quietly.

Dan stared at his transcript. “But she didn’t lose. Because it wasn’t admissible. Because Her Honour never opened the door.”

Zara closed her folder slowly. “She didn’t lie. She just didn’t let the truth expand.”

The professor stepped forward, voice calm but iron-edged.

“This is the part they don’t teach you early enough. That what you leave out can be more powerful than what you say. That omission is not deception – not in law – unless you cross the line. And Justice Brady knew where that line was drawn.”

“You’re Reading the Words Only”

The classroom had gone quiet again. Not out of boredom – but because something had shifted. The transcript pages sat still on desks. A few students had stopped typing. Zara’s highlighter hadn’t moved in two minutes.

The professor held the transcript in one hand, turning to a marked section with a deliberate gesture.

She read aloud once more, flatly:

“I didn’t want to kill him. I didn’t even want to hurt him. I just wanted to not be afraid anymore.”

Then she looked up.

“Now. You’ve all just heard that again. It’s the same sentence.”

She took a step forward.

“But you’re reading the words only, students. You’re not hearing the emotion of the trial.”

A beat. No one moved.

“You’re reading courtroom dialogue like it’s statute. Clean. Linear. But the jury didn’t hear it that way. They saw her. They watched her struggle to find those words. They felt the weight of everything she couldn't say."

Her tone softened – not gentle, but honest.

"You have the benefit of hindsight, footnotes, and Wi-Fi. They had twelve chairs, four days, and a woman telling them she was scared."

Dan stared at his transcript. Zara lowered her eyes. John – for once – said nothing.

The Final Reflection – Closing the Lecture

The classroom had fallen still.

Not the stillness of distraction or exhaustion, but the kind that came from everyone realising they'd just seen something larger than a case – and maybe even larger than law.

The professor glanced once more at the transcript in her hand, then set it down.

"Of course," she said quietly, "we'll never truly know what happened inside that jury room."

She looked out across the seminar table. No one moved.

"There's no transcript for that. No clean record of what was said. Only that they asked the judge a question:"

She walked to the board, writing slowly:

"Can we find her guilty, but recommend leniency?"

The words hung there, dry-erase and stark.

"And the judge told them no. That wasn't the law's question. The law didn't ask whether they felt for Ms Jarra. Or whether they wished it had gone differently."

She turned, voice quiet but precise.

"The law asked one thing: did they believe, beyond reasonable doubt, that she intentionally caused serious injury – without lawful excuse."

She paused.

"And they said no."

Another pause. Then she added:

"Which means Her Honour – then a young Legal Aid solicitor – did something extraordinary. She didn't beg for sympathy. She didn't plead for mercy. She stood there and walked the jury – word by word – through the wreckage. And she showed them that fear can be human and lawful. That truth can be messy and still matter."

The students watched her.

She stepped back and underlined the final word on the board:

REASONABLE.

Then:

"And she did it the only way that works – by telling the story with nothing to hide, and nothing to prove. Just belief."

The professor closed her folder, then looked up and addressed the class.

"Before we wrap, let me be clear about something. We've spent a lot of time examining the defence strategy in R v Jarra, and rightly so – it was nuanced, deliberate, and instructive. But we haven't discussed the Crown's role. That's not because they did anything wrong. Quite the opposite."

She paused, letting the room settle.

"The Crown prosecutors in this case fulfilled their duties with professionalism and integrity. Their role is to present the evidence fairly and to act in the public interest, not merely to secure a conviction. They followed their brief from the State of Victoria to the letter, ensuring that the proceedings were conducted justly."

She glanced around the room.

"Remember, the justice system relies on both the prosecution and the defence performing their roles ethically and competently. In R v Jarra, both sides did just that. The case serves as a powerful example of how our legal system is designed to function when each participant upholds their responsibilities."

The room was silent. Then the notebooks closed. Laptops clicked shut.

As the students began to leave, Priya lingered. She glanced once at the whiteboard, then to the professor.

"Do you think the jury wanted to convict her?"

The professor didn't answer right away.

She looked out the tall windows, voice softer now.

"I think they wanted to be allowed to. But they couldn't. Because Justice Brady didn't leave them any room for doubt."

A long beat. Then:

"And that's the difference between a good story… and a defence."

Justice Brady – For the Good of the Court

Judge Kimberly Brady glanced at her phone as it vibrated insistently against her polished oak desk. It was Monday morning, and the late autumn sun was painting the Melbourne skyline with golden hues. As she reached for her phone, her clerk's number flashed on the screen.

"Judge Brady here."

"Morning, Your Honour," the clerk said with a hint of urgency. "We've just received word from the Chief Justice's office. Judge Anderson broke his ankle during his Sunday bushwalk up at the Dandenong Ranges. He's out for at least six weeks."

Kimberley's eyebrows lifted. "Six weeks? That's a shame. I hope he's all right."

"He's in good spirits, Your Honour. But the problem is, he was scheduled to begin the Royal Children's Hospital fraud case this morning. It's been in pre-trial motions for months – motions are all done, jury selection has not yet occurred, and they're ready to begin testimony."

Kimberley's pulse quickened. "And the Chief Justice wants me to step in."

"Yes, Your Honour. Effective immediately. Everything's prepared; they're just waiting on you to take the bench."

Kimberley took a deep breath. The hospital fraud case. Allegations of misappropriated funds, accusations of extravagant spending by key figures within the hospital's administrative staff.

Her mind flickered, unbidden, to her own donations. The Brady Family's annual Good Friday contribution – $100, every year, without fail. A modest amount, but one that carried deep meaning.

"Very well. Please inform the parties, I'll be taking over. Give me twenty minutes to familiarise myself with the key points."

"Yes, Your Honour."

Kimberley set the phone down, her hand lingering over the receiver. The hospital had treated her youngest child. She remembered the sleepless nights, the frantic conversations with doctors, and the moment of relief when her child's condition had finally turned around. The donation had always been a symbol of gratitude.

Now, the hospital itself was at the centre of a scandal.

She reached for the case file, her fingers trembling slightly. Judge Anderson had handled all the pre-trial motions, so she would be starting at the deep end, with jury selection set to begin the next day. She had mere hours to prepare.

The timing was unfortunate. Good Friday was only days away, and the annual appeal was already running, with donations being read aloud on live television.

At that very moment, a young clerk working for the defence, reviewing donation readouts from the Good Friday Appeal, noticed a familiar name flash across the screen.

"Brady Family, Kimberley, Sarah, Josh & Nick – $100."

The clerk's eyes widened. He knew Judge Brady had been assigned to the Royal Children's Hospital case only hours earlier. He scribbled a note and rushed to his supervising attorney.

The defence lawyer did not hesitate. By midday, a formal Motion for Recusal was filed with the court clerk, citing reasonable apprehension of bias due to Judge Brady's personal donations to the hospital and her emotional connection to its mission.

The motion was delivered to Judge Brady's chambers by early afternoon, just as she was reviewing the details of the case.

Her clerk entered her office, expression tense.

"Your Honour, the defence has just filed a motion for recusal."

Kimberley looked up, her face tightening. "Already?"

"They acted fast. They must have caught your donation readout on the Good Friday Appeal."

Kimberley closed the case file, her heartbeat quickening. Duty first, she reminded herself. But as the motion rested on her desk, she couldn't ignore the weight of the implications.

Good Friday was days away. The appeal was in full swing. And now, her connection to the hospital was being called into question.

She had a decision to make.

The Motion Hearing

The courtroom was filled to capacity. Journalists, observers, and lawyers shuffled into their seats, the air thick with anticipation. The case against the hospital's administrators was high-profile, the allegations of fraud shocking enough to draw significant public interest.

Judge Brady took her seat on the bench, her gaze steady as she glanced at the assembled attorneys. The defendant, Johnathan Myers, sat beside his defence lawyer, his expression tense.

"Court is now in session. The matter before us is a motion for recusal filed by counsel for the defendant."

Judge Brady's voice was clear, professional. If she felt any unease, it didn't show.

The defence attorney, Mr Langford, rose to his feet. "Your Honour, the motion is straightforward. The defence respectfully requests your recusal from this case due to a reasonable apprehension of bias."

He held up a printed document. "The basis of our motion is the publicly documented donation made by Your Honour to the Royal Children's Hospital during the recent Good Friday Appeal."

A murmur spread through the courtroom. Judge Brady kept her expression neutral.

"Mr Langford, proceed."

"Yes, Your Honour. The donation was made in your family's name – Kimberley, Sarah, Josh & Nick – and read aloud during a public broadcast. The defendant believes that Your Honour's personal connection to the hospital, rooted in gratitude for the care provided to your own child, could influence your impartiality. It is not merely the financial donation, but the ideological and emotional commitment tied to it."

Mr Langford paused, then continued. "Your Honour's integrity is not in question. However, we submit that a reasonable person, aware of these facts, might reasonably apprehend that you could be subconsciously influenced in favour of the hospital."

Judge Brady nodded, her gaze steady. "And your requested relief?"

"We respectfully ask that Your Honour recuse yourself from presiding over this matter and that the case be reassigned to another judge before jury selection begins."

Judge Brady turned to the prosecutor from the Office of Public Prosecutions, Ms Carter. "Ms Carter, your response?"

Ms Carter rose, her tone calm but assertive. "Your Honour, the OPP opposes the motion. The donation referenced was a modest sum made during a public charity appeal. It does not indicate bias or partiality. Your Honour's integrity and ability to apply the law impartially are well-established."

"Further, Your Honour, the defendant has failed to establish a credible basis for bias. We contend that the motion is premature, speculative, and without merit."

She glanced at Mr Langford with polite precision. "Your Honour, I would simply note that my learned friend had previously raised concerns about timing related to the Good Friday Appeal. That matter was addressed and dismissed."

Judge Brady allowed the silence to stretch for a moment. "I will take the matter under advisement and issue my ruling before jury selection begins. Court is adjourned."

The Deliberation

Judge Brady sat alone in her chambers, the heavy mahogany door shut tight against the bustling sounds of the courthouse. The recusal motion lay open on her desk, alongside her own notes and relevant case law. The words of Mr Langford and Ms Carter echoed in her mind.

It was true. The donation had been made. It was not a large sum. Just a hundred dollars. But it wasn't about the money. It was about her connection to the hospital.

Kimberley leaned back in her chair, fingers clasped.

The annual Good Friday donation was a tradition – one rooted in gratitude, and perhaps something deeper: a sense of duty.

Her son had been born at thirty weeks. The care at the Royal Children's Hospital had been extraordinary – measured, steady, and quietly lifesaving.

The weeks that followed had been a blur of vigilance and hope.

It wasn't something she often spoke about. But she never forgot.

"I don't make the donation because I want to," Kimberley murmured aloud. "I make it because I feel I have to." She shook her head. "No, that's not right. I choose to. I want to. But perhaps I don't know if I could ever stop."

She tried to frame her thoughts through the lens of the law. Would a reasonable person, fully informed of the facts, apprehend that she might not bring an impartial mind to the case? Was her dedication to the hospital a bias?

"I am a reasonable person," she whispered. "I have taken an oath to uphold the law impartially. I have no personal stake in the outcome of this trial. The donation does not change that."

But the defence's argument lingered. What if her judgment, even unconsciously, leaned in favour of the hospital? What if her affection for the institution clouded her assessment of evidence, even in the smallest of ways?

Kimberley opened the case law she had pulled from her clerk's research. The precedent was clear. *Ebner v Official Trustee in Bankruptcy* (2000) reaffirmed that the test was not actual bias, but whether a fair-minded observer might reasonably apprehend bias.

She ran her fingers along the page. "The problem," she said to herself, "is that the observer does not see what I feel. I know my own integrity. I know that I am not biased. But the standard is not what I know – it's what others might perceive."

She sighed, her shoulders slumping. "If my connection to the hospital causes even the slightest doubt in the public's mind, then my presence on this case undermines justice."

For a moment, she considered stubbornly pushing forward. Why should she be disqualified from hearing a case simply because she had once benefited from the hospital's care? Wasn't her legal training meant to shield her from such emotional interference?

But it wasn't about her training. It was about perception.

She reached for her pen and began to write her ruling. By the time her clerk knocked on the door, she had finished. Her decision was ready.

Mark Ashbourne's Analysis

The camera panned to Mark Ashbourne, seated in his familiar leather chair on the *Today Show*. His glasses reflected the studio lights as he adjusted them with an air of authority.

"Good morning, everyone," Mark began, his voice rich with gravitas. "Today, we're talking about Judge Kimberly Brady's decision to recuse herself from the high-profile Royal Children's Hospital fraud case. And to be clear, this was a masterclass in judicial integrity."

He leaned forward, hands clasped. "Here's the thing. The law requires judges to be impartial – not just in reality, but in the perception of the public. Even the appearance of bias can erode faith in the judiciary. Judge Brady understood that."

A photo of Judge Brady appeared on the screen, her expression calm but resolute.

"Now, I've heard some folks say that her hundred-dollar donation was insignificant. And financially, sure, it is. But that's not the point. The point is that her donation was personal. It was tied to her family, her children, and a deep sense of gratitude towards the hospital. Whether or not she could rule impartially isn't even the real issue. It's whether a reasonable person would believe she could."

Mark's eyes narrowed, his voice growing more emphatic. "Judge Brady realised that her integrity wasn't under question. But public confidence in her impartiality was. And rather than fight the motion tooth and nail, she did the hardest thing a judge can do: she stepped aside."

Mark's tone shifted, a subtle, knowing smile crossing his face. "But here's the real gotcha moment, folks. And I doubt most people saw it coming."

He leaned in closer, his voice dropping slightly for emphasis. "Mr Langford's motion wasn't just about Judge Brady's donation. Sure, he used that angle because it was there, but the real play? Timing."

"Think about it," Mark continued. "Good Friday is this week. The hospital's appeal is everywhere – television, radio, newspapers. The public is inundated with emotional images of sick children, heartfelt pleas for donations, and praise for the hospital's incredible work. Potential jurors are being influenced every single day."

"Now, here's the twist," Mark said, his eyes gleaming. "During the hearing, Ms Carter from the OPP made a passing comment – one most people probably missed. She referred to Mr Langford's previous motion to delay the trial, noting that it was 'addressed and dismissed'."

Mark leaned back, a hint of respect in his tone. "Ms Carter is a sharp prosecutor, and her point was valid. She recognised that Mr Langford had raised timing concerns before and that this motion could be seen as a subtle attempt to revisit those arguments. Her observation was well-placed and appropriate for the situation."

"But here's the key point," Mark continued. "Judge Brady was never aware of Langford's strategy – nor would she be expected to consider it. Judges are bound to rule based on facts, not speculation or suspicions about motives. She made her decision based solely on the appearance of bias, as the law requires."

"What makes Langford's move so impressive is that he structured his argument around something Judge Brady couldn't ignore, even if others suspected there was more at play. By framing the motion solely on bias, Langford ensured that Judge Brady would have to rule on that issue alone."

"So, what happens next? The trial gets pushed, the Good Friday Appeal passes, and public sentiment cools. Mr Langford accomplished exactly what he wanted without ever having to say it."

Mark leaned back in his chair, his smile widening. "And if you ask me? That's the mark of a truly skilled advocate. Knowing when to pivot, when to press, and when to let the pieces fall into place."

He glanced directly into the camera, delivering his final thought with precision. "This isn't about Judge Brady's integrity or her impartiality. It's about leverage. And Mr Langford played his hand brilliantly."

James Brady – Powerplay

The late afternoon sun filtered through the skyscraper windows of the upper boardroom at Franks & Valentine, throwing gold slashes across the polished stone table. Up here, deals weren't just discussed – they were orchestrated, with the precision of a symphony no junior associate was allowed to hear.

David Harlan stood at the head of the table, a thick dossier in his hand, radiating the effortless authority that came from decades of winning. Around him, a small handful of senior partners sat in perfect silence.

The double doors swung open without ceremony.

James Brady entered first, flanked by Cal Whitmore and Evan Ross, his two most trusted lieutenants – not equals, but extensions of his will. All three wore silk-tailored suits that caught the afternoon light with a muted sheen. Their movements were economical, rehearsed without rehearsal. Predators in a boardroom of lions.

David's gaze flicked briefly to Cal and Evan but settled back on James. It was clear who had the power, and who borrowed it.

"You brought your crew," David said, voice dry but amused.

James took the seat directly across from him, Cal and Evan flanking him like sentinels. "You wanted this run right. That means we start building the war room now, not after the first shot's fired."

"James," David said, extending a hand with a polished smile. "Appreciate you making the time."

James took it firmly. "Always a pleasure," he said – the lie smoothly delivered, like a professional courtesy.

Across the room, an assistant – barely noticed – uncapped a crystal decanter and poured Johnnie Walker Blue Label into thick, cut-crystal tumblers. The scotch caught the golden sunlight and refracted it into tiny flames across the marble tabletop.

James accepted his glass with a nod.

"Franks & Valentine treating us right today," he said, swirling the liquid once, savouring the burn behind the cool. Cal and Evan did the same, though neither touched their glasses yet – they were here to watch, to listen, to measure.

David smiled thinly and slid the dossier across the table.

"Class action. Misleading disclosures. Early math puts the exposure north of two hundred million – possibly more, if the dominoes fall the way we think."

Cal was already flipping open a notepad, pen moving silently. Evan scanned the first few documents with the cool detachment of a field surgeon prepping for battle.

David continued. "It's high-risk. Big reward. We need someone who can control the chaos, who knows when to pull the trigger, and when to hold back."

"And when to burn everything down," Franklin Mayes added, tapping a manicured finger against the marble.

James opened the dossier slowly, page by page. Leaked memos, flawed audits, hidden fees – a trove of sins just waiting to be dragged into the light.

He didn't ask why he had been chosen. He already knew.

Franks & Valentine didn't want a clean win. They wanted a decisive one.

James closed the file with a soft snap, folding his hands lightly on the tabletop.

"And you boys…" – he let the words hang for a beat, surveying the room with a faint smile – "you're looking for a finder's fee."

The polite laughter was still dying down when David Franks leaned forward, resting his fingertips lightly on the dossier.

"Sixty-forty," he said casually, as if discussing the weather. "Our favour, of course."

The room went still, the words settling over the marble table like a drawn knife.

James continued, tapping the dossier with one finger. "You want me to put my name on this for forty? You want my team to build it, run it, carry it – for less than control?"

"You do good work – corporate deals, criminal pleas, lower court wins. Keeping CEOs out of mug shots and drunk drivers on the road. But this? This is a different game. You called us because when it gets this big, this dirty, you know you're out of your depth," James said, his words sharpened to a scalpel's edge.

Franks's eyes glinted, but he was weighing, calculating. Finally, he gave a reluctant nod.

"Fifty-two, forty-eight. Our favour." From James.

David Franks' brows twitched slightly. James noticed. He didn't stop.

"You'll run the client intake. You'll handle the interviews. You'll gather affidavits, coordinate signatures and manage the admin side."

James let the words settle, heavy and irreversible.

"We," he said, voice slicing through the room, "run the legal."

He looked around the table deliberately – daring any of the senior partners to speak. None did.

"We craft the filings," James continued. "We build the narrative. We argue the motions. We own the courtroom. We handle the PR. The media."

He gave a small, final smile – not warm, not cruel. Just absolute.

"You carry the buckets," James said. "We make the rain."

The words hung in the air, sharp as broken glass.

David Franks held his scotch tightly, the glass creaking faintly in his hand.

James moved toward the door, Cal and Evan falling into step beside him, a private phalanx of power in motion.

As they pushed through into the hallway, the city lights stretched out before them – cold, glittering, and ready.

James spoke casually, like a man making small talk after closing a deal that would ripple across the industry.

"Men," he said, slipping a hand into his pocket, "how about dinner?"

Cal raised an eyebrow.

"Where you thinking?"

James didn't hesitate.

"Flower Drum."

Cal gave a low chuckle. "Class move."

Evan smirked. "Might even let you pick the wine, boss."

James smiled thinly as the elevator doors opened with a soft chime.

"Tonight," he said, stepping inside, "we celebrate."

Allegra Preston – The Final Bow

The house was quiet except for the soft clinking of pots in the kitchen.

Sarah sat slouched on the couch, lazily flicking through Foxtel, not really paying attention.

In the kitchen, Kimberly was busy chopping vegetables, humming softly to herself.

Suddenly, Sarah's thumb froze.

Her eyes widened.

Mum! Mum, come quick!" she shouted, scrambling upright.

"Allegra's on the television! Oh gosh, it's *The Real Housewives of Melbourne*!"

Kimberly rushed in, tea towel still in hand, heart racing.

They both stared at the screen.

And there she was.

Allegra.

The screen showed a ballroom bathed in golden light, sparkling like a dream.

A crowd of long-standing ladies – Melbourne's old elite – stood poised and polished, whispering behind their hands.

Into that glittering world walked Allegra.

Her dress – shimmering silver, clinging perfectly – caught every glint of the chandeliers.

Her smile lit up the entire room.

She was breathtaking.

Sarah gripped Kimberly's arm, whispering, "Look at her, Mum… she's stunning."

On screen, the elegant old guard turned to look.

Their gazes sharpened like knives.

One of the grand dames stepped forward, her voice icy, clear even through the television:

"Allegra… you're not invited."

Sarah gasped.

Kimberly stiffened.

But Allegra didn't even blink.

She smiled – cool, dazzling, unstoppable.

She took one graceful step forward and said, her voice carrying across the ballroom:

"Darling, this is beautiful Brighton Way.

I'm invited to every party."

She leaned in just a little, playful and deadly all at once:

"And a modern girl doesn't wait for an invitation – she sees what she wants… and takes it."

The camera caught the stunned faces around her as Allegra swept past them, head high, claiming the night like it already belonged to her.

In the living room, Sarah and Kimberly burst into cheers, clapping and laughing through tears.

Their Allegra – beautiful, fearless, unforgettable – had just given the world her final bow.

And she had done it her way.

Kimberly Brady – The Apple and the Garden – The New Beginning

The late autumn sun filtered through the golden leaves of Gardens Close, casting a warm glow over the gravel paths nestled between Melbourne's Supreme and Magistrates' Courts. The air was crisp, carrying the subtle scent of eucalyptus, and the distant hum of city life was softened by the rustling trees.

Judge Kimberly Brady walked slowly, her robe folded neatly over her arm. Dressed in a pale silk blouse and a charcoal skirt, she exuded a quiet elegance. Her polished heels clicked softly against the stones as she sought a moment of tranquillity before the afternoon session.

A familiar voice interrupted her thoughts.

"Your Honour, you've dropped this."

She turned to see Paul approaching, a pristine red apple in his outstretched hand.

"I don't recall dropping an apple," she replied, a playful smile tugging at her lips.

"Consider it a gift," he said, his eyes reflecting a warmth that stirred memories.

She accepted the apple, their fingers brushing briefly. "Thank you, Paul."

They began walking together, the conversation flowing effortlessly, as if no time had passed.

"How have you been?" she enquired.

"It's been a journey," he admitted. "Helena passed a few years ago. It's been challenging, but the boys keep me grounded."

"I'm sorry to hear that," she said softly, her gaze meeting his with genuine empathy.

He nodded, the weight of loss evident in his eyes. "Christopher is now a third-year apprentice mechanic with Uncle Theo. Liam is in Year 12 at Broadmeadows High. They're growing up fast."

"You must be proud," she remarked, her voice tinged with admiration.

"I am," he replied, a smile breaking through the sombreness. "What about you?"

"Sarah started her first year in law at Melbourne Law School," she shared, pride evident in her tone. "And my boys are growing too – one in primary, the other just started high school."

They continued their stroll, sharing stories of family, memories, and the simple joys of life. The garden, with its serene ambience, bore witness to their reconnection – a testament to enduring bonds and new beginnings.

As they reached the edge of the gardens, Paul hesitated, gathering his thoughts.

"Kimberly," he began, his voice gentle, "would you like to continue this conversation over dinner?"

She considered for a moment, a smile playing on her lips. "There's a place called Okami in Hampton. They have a second sitting at eight p.m. Would that work?"

He smiled, a hint of nervousness in his eyes. "I don't know where that is, but I'll find it."

"Great," she replied, her smile widening. "It's a date."

Two Months Later

The sun rose slowly over the Melbourne suburbs, filtering soft amber light through the kitchen blinds. Judge Kimberly Brady stirred awake to the distant sound of clinking cups and laughter. As she wrapped her robe around her and padded barefoot down the hallway, the scent of raisin toast and coffee wrapped around her like a childhood memory.

In the kitchen, her daughter Sarah was perched at the counter with a cup of tea, a worn casebook beside her.

"Morning, Mum! You will not believe the hypo we discussed in study group last night," she said, eyes bright. "It was about a judge who eats Snickers bars in chambers every day and is sitting on a case between Big Chocolate and the Anti-Sugar Coalition. The judge said they loved all chocolate equally. It sparked a huge debate about impartiality."

"I remember getting that one in first-year ethics. The group split straight down the middle – half said 'Recuse,' the rest thought it only counted if the judge planned to eat the evidence."

"Mum, you like Snickers bars," Sarah said with a grin.

"Not enough to recuse myself," Kimberly replied, smiling into her coffee.

Kimberly raised an eyebrow with a smile, then asked softly, "And what was your decision, Sarah? Would you have recused?"

Sarah hesitated for just a beat, then nodded. "Yeah, I think I would have. Even if it was just chocolate – it's about trust, right?"

Kimberly watched her daughter for a moment, her smile deepening with quiet pride. She wanted to offer an answer, to guide her – but she held back.

"Good reasoning," she said instead. "Judges live and die on public confidence. But you'll learn, sometimes the hardest part of the law isn't knowing what's right – it's letting others find their own path to it."

Sarah blinked, then gave a small, thoughtful nod.

Kimberly said no more. She stood, rinsed her own mug, and placed it in the dishwasher. The hum of the machine hadn't yet begun, but the kitchen was already warming with light and the scent of early coffee.

A few quiet minutes passed – Sarah drying the bench with slow circles, Kimberly sorting through the papers on the table.

Then, still in her soft morning voice, Sarah spoke again. "Mum… you didn't really answer my question. Not completely."

Kimberly looked up, one brow raised.

Sarah offered a small smile. "I think I understand, though. It wasn't really about chocolate, was it? It was about the story the judge tells the room – what people need to believe about fairness."

Kimberly's lips curved into a smile, full of pride and affection. She nodded once, slowly.

It was enough. The spark of judgment was beginning to form in her daughter's eyes – and Kimberly had the wisdom to let it grow on its own.

"You're going to make a good lawyer, Sarah. The kind who hears more than just the words."

Sarah didn't respond, but the way she leaned her shoulder gently against her mother's on the way to grab her notes said everything. Two women, different stages of the same path, bound by respect – and a shared love for the law.

"Judges," Kimberly corrected playfully, sipping from her cup.

She paused for a moment, then touched Sarah's hand. "Paul and I are seeing each other tonight. I know it's still new, but… it matters. Could you look after Josh and Nick? Just for the evening?"

Sarah nodded, her smile softening. "Of course, Mum. Go enjoy it. Josh and Nick will probably be glued to their computer games anyway. We'll be studying tonight – or at least pretending to while 'Married at First Sight' plays in the background. Don't worry, Mum, I'll make sure they don't spend the whole night online."

Kimberly exhaled, letting the moment settle. Beneath the robe, behind the gavel, she was still a woman – still someone trying to balance justice, motherhood and the fragile hope of something tender.

The courthouse was quiet when she arrived. The security officers greeted her with the usual warmth, and she nodded politely, briefcase in hand. Her chambers were still, her clerk already seated at her desk reviewing documents.

"Good morning, Your Honour," said Clerk Dawson, standing briefly.

"Morning, Dawson. What are we running today?"

"Two preliminary hearings, then one full-day suppression matter in Courtroom 3. Also, the caterer wants to know your lunch order," Dawson said with a small smirk. "Chicken salad again?"

Kimberly glanced at the printed menu on her desk and smiled. "Tell them chicken salad. Some traditions are worth keeping. And Dawson – double-check the complainant's affidavit on the suppression hearing. Something about it seemed… forced."

"Already on it, Your Honour."

The court moved with its usual rhythm. Lawyers sparred gently, witnesses shuffled nervously, and Kimberly maintained her firm but compassionate demeanour. She broke for lunch at one fifteen p.m., slipping into the small lounge where her salad waited beside a bottle of mineral water.

Later that afternoon, after the gavel fell and transcripts were sealed, Kimberly stepped out into the crisp April air. Her car was parked inconspicuously, her robes tucked away, her hair now loose and casual. She checked her phone – a text from Paul.

"Paul: Table's ready. Quiet place. Discretion assured."

She smiled.

Paul was still an associate, working out of the Broadmeadow office, fifteen kilometres from the city. He never pushed for partnership or profile, but he'd built a steady, respected practice – mostly smaller criminal matters: drink driving, assaults, summary charges. Cases that didn't make news but mattered to real people. A country boy who had fought his way into Melbourne Law, he hadn't become what the city expected, but he had become someone solid.

They'd set the boundaries early. No lunches near the court, no coffee breaks where clerks might see. No blurred lines. If either of them crossed the ethics, it would be over – not from shame, but because they both knew the work mattered too much.

And yet, for all that constraint, there was room for warmth. They could hold hands under the table, share a quiet kiss in a dimly lit car park, laugh without whispering. There was affection, but not indulgence. Love with morals – the kind that breathes in careful spaces and still finds room to grow.

Kimberly drove with the windows down, letting in the scent of gumtrees and dusk. It was just dinner, just Paul. But sometimes, a normal day was all she needed to remind herself why she still loved the law – and life around it.

At exactly seven p.m., a quiet knock sounded at the front door. Sarah, now in a grey tracksuit with her hair up in a messy bun, answered with a grin.

"Hi, Paul. She's just finishing up. Come in."

The house smelled like dinner had recently been made – faint tomato and garlic notes still lingered. The living room was comfortably chaotic: Josh and Nick were sprawled across the rug, shouting at the screen as their avatars clashed in some brightly coloured video game. On the coffee table sat a half-eaten apple, a crumpled chip bag, and a can of Coke. A Current Affair murmured on the television in the background.

Sarah's laptop was open on the couch, her notes spread out neatly beside her. A tab was open to the University of Melbourne Law School library – her first-year readings visible in tight font. She had made it into Melbourne Law, something Paul, a country boy, quietly admired – and something even Kimberly hadn't achieved in her day, having studied at Monash instead. It was still a respected school – Kimberly had built a remarkable career from it, rising all the way to the bench. But Melbourne Law was seen as the highest rung, the most direct path to the top. Kimberly had wanted this for Sarah – a faster track, fewer barriers, a name that opened doors before she ever stepped through them. Sarah was already standing where many only hoped to begin. Court paperwork was on display – she'd clearly been reading up on real case files. Paul smiled faintly at the sight.

"Proper study setup," he said lightly.

She tilted her head, teasing. "Mum said you were already practising when I was in prep. That makes you, like, legal vintage." I've managed to highlight two paragraphs between sorting out snacks and mediating sibling battles."

She glanced at her screen, then added with a grin, "I can't imagine having to photocopy everything. Mum said you had to queue just to get textbook pages back when she was at Monash."

Paul smiled faintly. "We did. Ten cents a page, if you had the coins. And you never wanted to forget a footnote – it meant another walk back across campus the next day."

Paul remembered being not much older than Sarah, a boy from the country who came to Melbourne with a suitcase and a head full of ambition. Back then, if he needed a case note or textbook chapter, he had to race across campus to the library before it closed. Photocopying cost ten cents a page – and that was only if you had the right coins. He remembered queuing to use the noisy old machine tucked in the back of the library, carefully laying down his case notes one page at a time, hoping the copier wouldn't jam. Before that, he'd usually grab a quick dinner at the canteen – whatever was left on the hotplate. Often, a ladle of curry over rice or a meat pie and sauce, chased with a Coke from the vending machine. He'd eat with one eye on the clock, knowing he had less than an hour to make it across campus and copy what he needed before the library shut its doors.

Now, seeing Sarah – comfortable, engaged, connected – he realised just how different things were. She wasn't doing anything less than he had – just differently. She had the internet, a library that never closed, and real-time access to legal materials. But the spark in her eyes, the determination behind her study notes – those were the same. What had taken him photocopiers, vending machines, and lonely fluorescent nights, she now built in her own way – with Wi-Fi, siblings arguing in the background, and a soft-lit lounge room.

The biggest difference? She studied in front of a seventy-inch television, not a scratchy old portable with rabbit ears and a terrible picture. He used to split his focus between paragraphs and reruns of The A-Team, with a bag of chips and a warm can of Coke beside his photocopied pages. Yet the intention felt familiar – making do, building discipline out of distraction.

And Paul, rather than feeling outpaced by progress, felt quietly proud that she had these tools – and knew how to use them.

But somewhere, just beneath the pride, a quiet ache flickered. He had studied at Melbourne Law too – a country boy who'd made it through discipline, late nights and a long uphill climb. And yet, the career path that was supposed to open wide never quite did. Watching Sarah – young, connected, already on the upward track – he couldn't help but wonder if the law had always been more a staircase for some and a moving walkway for others.

A moment later, Kimberly appeared at the hallway's end, wearing a simple navy dress and a smile just for him.

"Sorry, I took too long choosing shoes," she said.

"Worth the wait," Paul replied, and she kissed Kimberly's forehead on the way out.

"Thank you."

Sarah waved them off, already half-lost in her notes.

They headed toward Mount Waverley, a few suburbs east, where the restaurants weren't flashy but served warm meals and offered privacy. Oakleigh had the best Greek food in Melbourne – but also half the Greek Bar Association. Kimberly didn't need sidelong glances or whispered questions. Not yet. Mount Waverley was just far enough.

They parked in front of a small bistro, tucked between a dry cleaner and a florist. Inside, it was quiet – wood panelling, soft lighting, the scent of lemongrass and fish sauce drifting through the air. The kind of place where no one looked twice at a judge and an associate quietly sharing a meal.

"I like this place," Paul said as they sat. "Comfortable, like someone's lounge room with wine."

"It's one of my favourites," Kimberly replied. "No linen napkins, no fuss, no risk."

She meant it. And Paul understood. This was how they stayed in balance – careful but honest, quiet but never hidden.

Halfway through their meal, a man at the bar with the kind of unsteady posture that suggested he'd had more than a few beers stood up and made his way toward their table. His voice came first – loud, edged with frustration.

Paul's body shifted subtly. He put down his cutlery and straightened, instantly alert.

Kimberly didn't flinch, but her voice was quiet and direct. "Paul. Let me handle this."

The man stopped at the side of their table. His tone was sharp now, words slurred but fuelled by long-held resentment.

"Rodney Glass," he said. "You gave me five years. Five years. You know how hard that was?"

Kimberly's face changed – not fear, but professional focus. "Mr Glass," she said evenly. "I do remember your case. The court considered a range of eight to ten years. You should have received ten. But we accepted your counsel's mitigation – particularly your daughter's ADHD – and sentenced you to eight, with five on the bottom. Your daughter needed you then. She needs you now."

Rodney blinked. The edge in his voice faltered, just for a moment. "She's doing well…"

Kimberly's voice softened only slightly. "That is good. But this – confronting me here, like this – is highly inappropriate."

She continued, "If someone reports this to your parole officer, it could be viewed as a breach. You know what that means. How would that help your daughter now?"

Rodney glanced at Paul, then back at Kimberly. His jaw twitched, but he said nothing. After a long pause, he muttered something under his breath and turned, heading toward the door.

Paul looked over, his expression still tense.

"I'm not allowed to defend my girlfriend now?" he said, his voice low but tight. "That man walked up to you in public, angry, aggressive. This should be reported."

Kimberly looked at him, steady and calm. "Paul. Mr Glass does not deserve a custodial sentence for a missed parole breach – and he's had a little too much to drink. But I know why you stepped in."

She gave a small, honest smile. "Of course, you're allowed to defend your girlfriend. That's what people do when they care." Her tone softened, but remained composed. "But if we report this, it becomes part of the public record. And once that happens, everyone – everyone in the Bar Association – will know."

Paul's shoulders eased back slowly. But what rattled him wasn't just the man – it was the weight of what could have happened.

He imagined the report – a formal complaint, police involvement, statements. His name and Kimberly's on file together. He imagined it landing quietly in the inboxes of the senior partners at his firm. The next Friday, David Franks and the other partners would be in the lounge with their Blue Label scotch – the one they never opened for juniors like him. Franks would lean back in his chair, smirking as he raised a glass: 'Look at him – in his forties, still running traffic lists and drink-driving pleas. Built the firm half its billables in the lower courts, and he still thinks dating a judge gets him to the top. The only bench he'll ever see is the one in her kitchen. The only way he'd ever get near the bench is if he started dating one.

They'd all laugh – not because it was clever, but because it was cruelly true. And Paul could see it – the Friday afternoon ritual, the partners circled with their Blue Label poured, no junior in sight. He wasn't part of their world, never would be. The joke wasn't just about him dating a judge. It was about class, ambition, and the audacity to reach above your rung. The only bench he'd ever be near was the one he was dating. Never by merit. Never by appointment. And yet here he was – beside her. Not because he earned a seat in their world, but because she'd made space in hers.

Paul would laugh, too, of course. Because not laughing would mean explaining. And no one wanted that.

He looked at Kimberly across the table, really looked. The silence between them wasn't cold – just real.

He gave a faint laugh, not bitter, but honest. "And here I am, playing the protector. But you're the one who carries the decisions. The robe. The ghosts."

Kimberly's voice, when it came, was low and warm. "You see me. That's more than most ever try."

She reached across the table, not for words, but for connection. Her fingers brushed his.

"Paul," she said softly, "I'm dating you because you're kind. Because you're ethical. Because you don't care about status, and you treat people like they matter. That includes me."

She paused, letting it settle.

"The boys are looking forward to the footy with you on Saturday. Josh has been laying out his scarf since Wednesday. Nick's been telling everyone he's going to the MCG – the Melbourne Cricket Ground – with you this weekend. You're not just good to me – you're steady, safe, real. They feel it too. That's why they want you at the footy, not just for the game – but because they trust you. And I see that."

Then she smiled, not like a judge, but like a woman. "So let's forget the partners with their Blue Label and smug little rituals. They don't get to define who deserves to be beside me. I do."

She leaned forward slightly, her voice just above a whisper. “Kiss me, please.”

Her words landed not like flattery, but absolution – as if she had seen every imagined failure in his mind and chosen him anyway. Paul didn’t hesitate. He leaned across the table and kissed her softly on the lips – not rushed or hidden, but with quiet conviction. For a moment, there was no courtroom, no robe, no past. Just them.

The End